MIND CHANGE

The Overcomer's Handbook

THOMAS A. JONES

MIND CHANGE

The Overcomer's Handbook

SECOND EDITION

DPI
DISCIPLESHIP
PUBLICATIONS
INTERNATIONAL

1-888-DPI-BOOK
www.dpibooks.com

All Scripture quotations, unless indicated, are taken from
the HOLY BIBLE, NEW INTERNATIONAL VERSION.
Copyright @ 1973, 1978, 1984 by International Bible Society.
Used by permission of Zondervan Publishing House.
All rights reserved.

MIND CHANGE: The Overcomers Handbook
SECOND EDITION

'1997 by Discipleship Publications International
One Merrill Street, Woburn, MA 01801

All rights reserved.
No part of this book may be duplicated, copied, translated,
reproduced, or stored mechanically or electronically without specific,
written permission of Discipleship Publications International.

Book Design by Chris Costello
Printed in the United States of America

ISBN 1-57782-022 3

To Sheila
who has stood by me for twenty-seven years,
overcoming and helping me
to do the same

Contents

Acknowledgments

When I began to jot down short thoughts more than five years ago to help me get through some tough days, I had no vision for a book like this. However, as those thoughts made a difference in my life and in the lives of others with whom I shared them, I was given much encouragement to think about writing a book. I am indebted most of all to my wife, Sheila, and our three daughters—Amy, Bethany and Corrie for their daily affirmation, support and prayers. Also, my mom and dad, Tom and Violet Jones, although hundreds of miles away, certainly urged me on in many important ways.

Right behind these loved ones is my other "family" here at Discipleship Publications International—our awesome staff members who have given me their hearts as we have worked together for the last two years. It is a joy, even on the hard days, to come to work with all of you. Thanks for putting up with me, especially after 3:00 p.m. when I'm sometimes unintelligible.

I owe a real debt of thanks to Randy McKean, Wyndham Shaw, Gordon Ferguson and Dan Bathon—all leaders in my life who have believed in me and given me vision. I thank God that he has raised up so many people like these in our generation—people who love warmly, see clearly and challenge prophetically. Without them my efforts to overcome would not be where they are today.

I must also say thank you to some of the courageous overcomers who have inspired me by staying in the race in spite of all kinds of challenges—those in the physically challenged ministry of the Boston church and others like Greg Gaumond, Ron Cicerchia, Angie Chandler, Joyce Conn, Erica Kim, and some special disciples married to non-believers who have my deepest respect. Your lives do make a difference!

And finally, I give thanks to God, who is the one this book is really about. All ultimate overcomers will be praising him for eternity. His grace is what makes us winners. I see others trying to overcome without him. I would not want to be in their shoes.

Preface to the Second Edition

When I wrote the first edition of this book more than two years ago, I did so with a bit of fear and trepidation. I knew that the things I included were most helpful—even powerful—to me. I felt in many ways that they had saved my life. But I just wasn't sure that others would find them equally helpful. After all, we are individuals and different things catch our attention and resonate in our experience. It is not unusual for me to see a movie with someone and have a totally different opinion of its impact. I wondered if the same would be true of this book.

However, the feedback I have received has assured me that the things I wrote about did touch a nerve with thousands of others. This is now our fourth printing, and I have heard from people from many continents who tell me the ideas I shared were powerful for them as well. I remember one man to whom I was serving a cup of water at a rest stop for a bike-a-thon. He said, "Your book didn't just give me a mind change. It gave me a life change." I was humbled and encouraged.

Just recently I was handed a copy of the new German translation of *Mind Change* which was initiated and produced entirely by German Christians. It was a strange feeling to see something I had written in a language I cannot speak, but it was a reminder to me that God is able to do far more than we ask or imagine.

Chapters Six, Seven, Eight and Thirteen are new chapters that were not in the first edition. I pray that the ideas found in these chapters will give some additional insights that help you renew your mind, increase your faith and overcome whatever obstacles there may be in your life.

Two years after publishing the first edition, I am more convinced than ever that right thinking leads to right actions and real victories, regardless of what issues are in our lives.

Boston, U.S.A.
New Year's Eve 1996

Preface to the First Edition

You are about to read a sentence that I never thought I would write. Here it is: *Multiple sclerosis is one of the best things that has ever happened to me.* When I first said that to myself, it seemed like a miracle.

I hated the disease. I fought it. I resented it. I looked at the people who didn't have it, and I wondered why in the world I did. I would think about all the walks I couldn't take, all the tennis and golf I couldn't play and the high-energy dad I could no longer be. I would wake up in the morning and think, *If this is the way life is going to be, I'm not sure I want it.* I would pray about it but would lose faith even as I prayed.

However, things changed in me, and MS has become one of my most important teachers in God's university of life. Sure, I still have some ambivalent feelings about it. I struggle when I watch some of you spike a volleyball. I long to cast it out when all my energy is gone by the middle of the day. But I know in my heart of hearts that God has used it to change my character and to show me something *you* need to learn just as much as I did: *We must be overcomers, and with God's help we can be—whatever the challenge.*

This is not a book just for the physically challenged. It is a book for *the challenged* and that means *all* of us. It is a book for people who need to overcome fear, loneliness, depression, insecurity, discouragement, guilt, despair, anxiety, resentment, ingratitude, persistent problems with sin, and other challenges too numerous to mention.

In part one I have attempted to dramatize some of the situations we find ourselves in where overcoming is clearly the need. This section is intended to draw our attention to the very real challenges life brings and help us get in touch emotionally with the need to find powerful attitudes that will enable us to overcome.

In part two we examine some basic and potent principles revealed in Scripture for facing the tough situations in life. This is the meat of the book and the part you will need to study carefully.

Part three contains "power thoughts" I have found to replace the negative thinking that naturally comes in tough times. If you cheat and skip to this section, looking for a *shortcut*, you will get *shortchanged*. The book is not that long. Get the principles first. Then part three will mean much more to you.

While your difficulties and mine are often very different, they are also remarkably similar. I pray that some of the lessons I'm learning and sharing with you here will help you. In turn I hope you will write me about your progress and your victories. I'm still in school and need all the good teachers I can find.

Nothing in this book or any book, including the Bible itself, will take away life's problems and challenges. But there is one thing that is certain: With God's grace, truth, power and presence, *we can overcome!*

PROBLEMS

The following stories are fictional
. . . or are they?
Actually, they describe life as it really is
and hopefully will remind us why we must all learn
from God to be overcomers.

Brian

Spiritual Discouragement

Brian Morley struggled out of bed, stumbled across the room, put on his glasses and walked to the kitchen. Outside it was dark and rainy, and he could almost feel the gloom seeping in through the open window. At least the coffee was ready, thanks to a timer that had started the morning brew thirty minutes earlier. One needed to be grateful for small things, he told himself.

He poured a cup, held it in one hand and gathered a worn leather Bible and small notepad in another. Walking to the next room, he sat down on a sofa.

> *Where should I begin?*
> *These times haven't been very good lately.*
> *I'm not feeling very victorious.*

Morley had become a disciple of Jesus four years earlier after his wife had been met by some women in the neighborhood. At first, he had been skeptical of her interest; but after she was baptized, he attended some of the studies with her, met some men he could relate to and discovered there was a lot in the Bible he had never known about. He had confessed his faith and been baptized on a Friday night in a lake near their home, and he had never once regretted the decision.

This morning, peering down at his Bible through bleary eyes, he still did not regret it, but had to admit something was not going as it should be. He was discouraged and that discouragement had become rather consuming in the last few weeks. For at least a year he and Karen had poured themselves into making some kind of spiritual impact in the neighborhood and their town. Several people had shown interest, only to back away when it became clear that being a disciple involved something more than "normal" religion.

Is it me?

Do I just not know how to connect with people?

I've prayed a lot. Do I just not have the right kind of faith?

I don't want to quit. But I have to admit I'm tired.

Sure, we have some great friends in the church.

Yes, our marriage is better than before, although it's been a bit tough lately.

Yes, the kids are getting something they wouldn't have gotten without the kingdom.

But trying to keep up with all the ministry needs while not seeing much result and getting lots of new pressures from work is wearing on me.

I see guys at work who aren't Christians, and they look like they are having more fun than I am. That doesn't seem right.

He turned the pages of his Bible, read a few verses from one of the gospels, offered up a few obligatory prayers, and went outside to get the morning paper, feeling no new power from his spiritual exercise.

❧

Brian Morley is a disciple, but he faces some real challenges. Will he let them beat him down? Will he accept his situation as part of the normal experience of a disciple? Will he eventually give up his commitment and go back to pursuing success, leisure and security? Or will he press through the challenges, overcome them and reclaim the joy that he and Karen knew when they first came into the kingdom? Will he get conviction that God did not send Jesus Christ to bring us into the spiritual doldrums, and will he fight until he has found the abundant life that the Bible describes? Will he humble himself and get the help offered by others who have been right where he is? Will he be overcome by discouragement and faithlessness, or will he experience a mind change and be an overcomer?

What would you do if you were Brian? What would you tell Brian if you were his friend?

Teresa

Non-Christian Spouse

Teresa Merullo looked at the calendar. June 27 would be the twelfth wedding anniversary for her and husband John. She wanted to feel some things she could not feel. She wanted to feel thankful and festive. She wanted to feel excited. She wanted to have a quiet dinner somewhere and be able to reminisce about all the great years. But these had been twelve tough years.

John did not hit her now as he did before. His worst moments were his tirades against the church, but at least the blows were now only verbal. He did more things with her and the kids than in the past, and he had turned down a good bit of overtime lately to be with them, but his attitude toward the church had remained unchanged for two years. He complained relentlessly about how much time she was on the phone with disciples, how many meetings she went to, and how all the church was after was their money.

Last year on their eleventh anniversary he had taken her on a nighttime cruise around the harbor, but the night had ended in a huge argument about her commitment to the church. Looking at the calendar, she wondered if this year would be more of the same and if she, once again, would be crying herself to sleep.

God had blessed her with some great friends in the king-dom. She had never had people in her life like Isabelle and Gloria. Many of the brothers took a special interest in her kids, showing them men can be godly. But sometimes she didn't know if she could stay with it. Why couldn't she have what most of the other women in the church had? She had prayed so much for John, but nothing seemed to change. The disciples had tried all kinds of different things to befriend him, but at his best he was evasive and at his worst he was downright rude.

❧

What will happen to Teresa? She doesn't have an easy life. Will she finally give in to self-pity? Will she blame God for not blessing her like he blesses others? Will she give up on John and blame him for ruining her life? Or will she get her focus back on Jesus who didn't have it easy either? Will she realize that God has done most of his great work in the midst of adversity? Will she say, "This is tough, but I have the most important thing—a relationship with God, and I will not stop sharing it"?

Will Teresa be overcome by a hardened husband, a dis-appointing marriage and an ongoing struggle, or will she keep her faith and be one of those heroes of whom the world is not worthy?

What would you do if you were Teresa? What would you tell Teresa if you were her friend?

J.B.

Tragic Accident

Six months ago J.B. Oliver was the star center fielder for his corporate softball team. A three-sport letterman in high school, a starting cornerback in college and a eight-year veteran of the corporate softball league, he had lost a few steps since his undergraduate days, but last summer could still track down a fly ball with the best of them and could park his share over the fence when at bat.

But all that was before the accident. It happened one evening on his way home from work. A tractor-trailer swerved to miss a car, and suddenly there was chaos. Fifteen cars piled up. There were no fatalities and no serious injuries, except one—J.B. was paralyzed from the waist down.

Seven years ago and a year out of college, he had run into one of his old classmates who got him interested in a Bible study. Five months later he had made the decision to be a disciple. Two years later he was married to a great Christian woman. Eighteen months later they had a beautiful baby boy, and J.B. had dreams of playing ball with him forever. He couldn't have been happier.

God blessed their ministry and they helped several other couples become disciples. His athletic skill enabled him to make friends easily, and he used it to get men to consider the gospel.

Now it was a whole new ball game. J.B. struggled to define himself. Before, he spent hours of fun on the field or the court. He was the life of the party, the guy everybody wanted to be with. Now he spent hours of pain in rehabilitation, asking himself, "Why me? Why now?" Before, he was the take-charge guy in most any situation. Now he had to watch as his wife did things for him that he could no longer do.

His company has told him they still value him and have a place for him, but it's obvious he can't be flying out of town several days a week, and he can already sense a change of attitude from his coworkers. There used to be respect. Now he feels their sympathy.

&

What will become of J.B.? Will he get bitter about the hand life dealt him? Will he let his disappointment drive him to give up on God or to accuse God of cruelty? Will he hang on spiritually but lose all vision of God doing anything great with him? Or, while naturally grieving his loss, will he say "my name is still written in heaven—and in that I rejoice"? Will he struggle with his new situation in prayer and in discipling until he finds a new place where he can be used? Will he, in his disability, become a much more inspiring person to others than he ever was with all his talents?

No healthy person would ask to be in J.B.'s situation. But it happens to hundreds of people every year. How will this disciple handle it? Will he find resources from God he once knew about only intellectually and go on to be a hero to his wife, son and dozens of others who will come to know him? Will he learn to pray like never before and learn to trust in God's Spirit more than man's flesh? Will he be overcome by a "senseless tragedy" or will he overcome tragedy with faith?

What would you do if you were J.B.? What would you say to him if you were his friend?

Jana
Unruly Thoughts

What is wrong with me?
Why can't my mind just leave me alone?
Where do these thoughts come from?
Why can't I do something to shut them down?

Jana Blackwell was sure that she had asked herself these questions at least five thousand times. She had become a disciple of Jesus ten years ago, but it had not been a smooth ride.

What frustrated her the most was the fact that externally things in her life had really gone very well, but she still had all these battles in her mind. Her parents had not been reactive to her decision to leave their traditional religion. Her mom had actually been quite open and was even now continuing to study the Bible. Her career in the biotech field had advanced quickly. She had always been blessed with good roommates and friends who loved her and now was engaged to someone who was respected and appreciated.

I should be happy. I should have peace of mind.

And yet the thoughts never really left her, at least not for very long.

You can't really love God. You don't even know what love is.

Others talk about how God is their best friend, but you have so much trouble feeling close to him.

You have many Christian friends, but you really don't belong.

You are faking it. You don't have what they have.

Just how long do you think David will put up with someone who has your problem?

People tell you how much you've helped them, but you can't even help yourself.

She had been open with others. She had tried a Christian counselor. Sure, she did get some help, but she could never seem to get over the hump. She could never seem to break free of these thoughts that were like chains around her neck.

She would have weeks and months where things would go much better. She would give of herself and make a difference in the lives of others. She would start to think these nagging thoughts were a thing of the past, only to go through some experience that would set them in motion all over again. Sometimes she would be sitting in a church service listening to powerful preaching only to hear, *You can never have conviction like this.* Or she might be in a group where others were sharing how God was working in their lives, and the thought would come, *Can you really believe this? Isn't a lot of this just coincidence?*

❧

How will Jana's story end? Will she conclude that the Bible works for some people but can't be totally true because it doesn't work for her? Will she decide that trying to be spiritual just creates too much psychic pain and look for more comfortable options? Will she muddle through the weeks and months, never really happy but afraid of what will happen if she leaves God?

Or will she decide that everybody has problems and challenges and that hers is just one more that must be faced? Will she be perplexed but not allow that to keep her from staying wholeheartedly with God and his plan? Will she focus on the promises of God again and again until one day her confidence in them dwarfs those negative thoughts that come from out of the darkness?

What would you do if you were Jana? What would you do if peace of mind did not come easily for you? What advice would you give her if she were a friend of yours?

Frank
Death of a Loved One

A few burnished leaves fell softly at Frank Vaughn's feet as he sat quietly on the hillside of Northridge Cemetery. At first only a single tear emerged and traveled down his face, but then moments later, as he gazed at the grave below him, he was weeping grievously. The memories of nine years with wife Sue flashed across the screen of his mind.

Oh, how he missed her. They had their scrapes and bumps like even in the best of marriages, but the truth was they had one of the best of marriages. They were devoted to each other. They helped each other through a hundred hard times. Sue had helped him come to faith and then she had lovingly supported him as he grew into a strong spiritual leader for her and the kids.

When she had told him about the lump the x-rays revealed in her breast, he had confidently said, "God will provide. With his help, you'll beat this." And he had believed that. He had believed right up until the very last. He was sure that God simply would not let Sue die—not now, not while she was having such an impact for him, not while her small children needed her so much, not while he needed her so much.

But then she died. She died a slow and difficult death for her, for Frank, for the children, for her parents and for a church full of loving brothers and sisters. She died heroically.

Thank God for that. She died sharing her faith until the end. She was an inspiration. That's what everyone said at the memorial service.

> In all things God works for the good of those who love him and are called according to his purpose.

How many times had Frank gone back to those words in the last six weeks? At times he held on tightly to them. Most everyone said he was holding up really well through all this. But then there were times, especially after he would put the kids to bed, when he would go out in the backyard, look up and say, "Why? Why? Why?" There were those mornings when he would wake up and reach over to put his arm around Sue, only to come back to reality and then pound his hand in grief on the bed.

Before the cancer, Frank was very close to a decision to leave his career and enter a full-time role in ministry with the church. Sue had been so excited. It was a dream come true to her. She loved nothing more than studying with others and helping them find God's plan. And just when they were so sure they knew what God's specific plan was for them, the illness changed everything.

❦

Now what will happen? Will Frank let his disappointment and grief disable his faith? Will his convictions waver? Will he not be sure anymore of just what God wants? Will he be afraid to trust again? Or will he hold to the promise that in all things God works for good, and will he stay with it until he sees how God fulfills that promise? Will he rejoice that Sue is with the Lord and do everything he can to get himself, his children and many others to that same destination?

What would you do if you were in Frank's shoes? How would you counsel him?

Carmen

Persecution from Family

Carmen Ortiz dabbed the ugly cut with a wash cloth. It was just below her left eye and was most tender to the touch. What hurt her even more, however, was that this nasty wound was created by a blow from her father.

Raised in a rather poor family and with two brothers who had already done jail time, Carmen was the girl who made good and made everybody proud. Blessed with a good mind and a drive to achieve, she had not only been the first in her family to go to college, but she eventually graduated with the highest honors, winning some large grants for graduate school.

In the midst of her pursuit of a law degree and with dreams of an exciting career, she met some disciples of Jesus and was immediately attracted to their commitment and zeal for God. Even as a little girl, she had always longed to know God better, and now she was drawn to these people who had made him the real priority of their lives.

As right as their approach seemed and as much as they were able to reinforce it with passages from the Bible, several things gave her pause. First was her own religious background. Her parents, in one sense, were very devoted to it, and she had never been able to see herself in any other church—although she had long felt that something big was missing in her experience. Second was the surprisingly angry reaction she found among many fellow students to her new Christian friends. She noticed that those who were serious disciples had no small amount of abuse heaped on them. She never doubted that she could stand up under such treatment, but she wondered if she needed to put herself in that position. Finally, there were her goals for education and career—would they be compatible with a radical commitment to God?

The challenges were real, but Carmen wanted God's will more than comfort or ease, and six months before this dreadful day, she had confessed Jesus as Lord and had been baptized in his name. But then it proved even tougher than she had thought. Not one to hide anything, Carmen had freely shared with her family about her new commitment, and their reaction was distressing. Her mother became hysterical every time they spoke on the phone, and her father's rage could be felt 800 miles away.

She fought through depression, devoting at least an hour or more every day to Bible reading and prayer and joining others in her new group who were out sharing their faith. The abusive reactions she had once only observed now came personally to her. Her roommate chastised her for hurting her family and jeopardizing her future career. A trusted professor brutally blasted her new faith as "a bunch of fundamentalist garbage." Students she had once studied and partied with, now turned a cold shoulder to her as she invited them to Bible discussions. But the crowning blow came when she finally went home for a holiday. For days her mother wept, and her father raved and ranted.

How could you do this to us?
How could you leave the church we raised you in?
How can you show such disrespect for us?
Is this where all your fancy education is leading
you—to show utter contempt for those who love
you most?

She prayed constantly, asking God to give her patience and understanding and, most of all, a gentle spirit. Except for a few outbursts which she apologized for, she felt good about her responses. But then on her last day home, just hours before she was to catch a plane back to school, her father became violent. Standing in the kitchen, he threw his coffee cup against the wall, knocked over a vase of flowers on the table and then walked across the room and struck her with the back of his hand. She had seen him strike her brothers before, but he had never come close to hitting her.

Now as she stood looking into the mirror and trying to get her face in some kind of shape for the trip back to school, her heart was heavy. At one time her mother and father had been so proud of her. Now they were totally ashamed of her. She loved God, but why did following him have to be so hard?

When she began her Bible studies, her friend Glendora had written in her Bible a verse from Jeremiah. It said God has a plan to prosper you and not to harm you. Could she still believe that?

❧

What will Carmen do? The opposition in her life is fierce. Will she give in? Will faith be conquered by feelings? Will she seek an escape from the pain? Or will she decide that her experience is not that different from the man she now calls Lord? Will she find in him the strength to overcome?

If you were Carmen, how strong would your convictions be? If you were her friend what advice would you be giving?

Philip
Depression

Outwardly Philip Dewitt looked like a guy who had it together. Throughout his life he had always been a success. Outstanding student. Responsible employee. Good husband and father. But inside him, things were happening that few people would have guessed. Seven years ago he started having lunch regularly with a friend from work who introduced him to a deeper understanding of the Bible. Raised in a religious home, he was always superficially spiritual—it fit with his "good guy" image. But he had never known any Christian with the kind of relaxed *and* joyful intensity that he found in his friend Roger.

Their studies went on for four months, and Philip and his wife Nancy eventually began attending church with Roger. A month after that, both confessed faith in Jesus and were baptized on the same day. Philip had always been plagued by negative thinking and a tendency toward depression, but he fully expected that his new venture into discipleship would bring a complete change in all that. It didn't.

Two years after he became a disciple, during a week when he was struggling more than usual with low feelings, Philip's boss called him in. Pleased with his outstanding work, he announced a promotion for Philip along with some "exciting new opportunities." Philip knew he should have been thrilled, but inside there was doubt and a sinking feeling. Somewhere within him someone was rolling the negative tapes, and during the next seventy-two hours they blared mercilessly into his mind.

> *People are always overestimating you.*
> *No one knows what you are really like.*
> *This time you will surely disappoint them.*
> *Other people will be questioning why in the world*
> *you were put in this role.*
> *Competitors will laugh when they hear about this.*
> *Even your wife will have a hard time supporting*
> *you.*

What had been in the past a tendency now became a full-blown expression of what some people have called "living death." Philip fell into a deep depression that would persist off and on for years. For a while, he kept up a pretty good front with others but he couldn't hide it from Nancy. He felt worthless, useless and powerless. He had no energy, no confidence, and had difficulty making the smallest decisions. On top of it all, he felt ashamed that such a thing was happening in his life.

Picking up his Bible one morning and turning through the Psalms—about the only part of the Scripture he could bear to read—his eyes fell on Psalm 88:

> For my soul is full of trouble
> and my life draws near the grave.

I am counted among those
    who go down to the pit;
  I am like a man without strength.
I am set apart with the dead,
  like the slain who lie in the grave,
whom you remember no more,
    who are cut off from your care.
You have put me in the lowest pit,
    in the darkest depths (Psalm 88:3-6).
But I cry to you for help, O Lord;
    in the morning my prayer comes before you.
Why, O Lord, do you reject me
    and hide your face from me?
From my youth I have been afflicted and close to
      death;
I have suffered your terrors and am in
    despair.
Your wrath has swept over me;
    your terrors have destroyed me.
All day long they surround me like a flood;
    they have completely engulfed me.
You have taken my companions and loved ones
      from me;
    the darkness is my closest friend
      (Psalm 88:13-18).

"The darkness is my closest friend." Many times in the next four or five years Philip would think about that line. Sadly, it described so well what he felt. But again and again through those years he would cry out "Why?" *Why is this my state of mind? Why couldn't the Psalmist get out of it, and why can't I?* Eventually he opened it all up to others. Like Job's friends they checked him out for sin, but could find nothing other than the ongoing battles all disciples face.

He would go through months where things would improve, but then a new hit of some kind would plunge him back into the pit. He lived life like a man walking on thin ice, always wondering when the next break would come.

He wanted to die, but he hated that he thought like this. Somewhere he read about someone who was going through a depression who got through it by holding tightly to the "grace of daily obligation." That helped. He looked at Nancy and the kids and the brothers and sisters in the church, and he kept going. But he was still like a weak man carrying a heavy load.

At times his faith was a comfort, and he especially drew hope from the Psalms, for here were spiritual men who seemed to share his feelings. But at times his faith seemed a curse. "It almost seems it would be easier to bear this if I weren't trying to hold to faith in a good God," he told a friend. "Why would a good God let me feel this low? Why won't he pull me up out of it? How long will he let this go on?"

But then he would feel ashamed of his tirades and anger against God, and his guilt and shame would drive him deeper into his pit. "What will become of me? What will become of me?" Philip would sometimes sob as tears streamed down his face.

❧

What *will* become of Philip? Does he have any hope? Does he have any choices left? Will he leave the church? Will he turn to alcohol? Will he get through this but lose all faith in God? Will his depression someday leave, only to be replaced by bitterness and doubt? Will he take his life?

Or will he go through this and emerge as an overcomer? Will he tie a knot at the end of his faith and hold on, seeing God use him even in the midst of his struggle? Will he one day mentally stand above his depression (that "living death") and laugh at it and taunt it as Paul laughs at and taunts death itself in 1 Corinthians 15? Will he find in the words of Corrie ten Boom that "no pit is so deep that God is not deeper still"? Will he one day say, "Thank God for the depression because of what I learned coming through it"? Is such a turnaround possible?

You may never feel what Philip felt. You may wonder why anybody would, but what if you did? Or what if Philip were your friend sitting in your living room still battling his depression? What would you say? How would you help him?

PRINCIPLES

Chapter One
To Him Who Overcomes

"'I have told you these things, so that in me you may have peace. In this world you will have trouble. But take heart! I have overcome the world '" (John 16:33).

"He who has an ear, let him hear what the Spirit says to the churches. To him who overcomes, I will give the right to eat from the tree of life, which is in the paradise of God" (Revelation 2:7).

"To him who overcomes and does my will to the end, I will give authority over the nations. . ."
(Revelation 2:26).

G od has a plan for our lives—a plan to prosper us and not to harm us (Jeremiah 29:11), but obstacles stand in the way. Troubles appear on the right and on the left. Enemies oppose us. Dreams get shattered. Disappointments come. God's will cannot be done in our lives without struggle. Battles must be fought. Hardships must be endured. Solutions must be sought and found. To accomplish God's plan and fulfill our purpose, we must *overcome* all kinds of obstructions and impediments. Scripture makes it clear that we must *all* be overcomers.

Simply put, overcoming takes place whenever you move

*ahead and do the will of God in spite of circumstances (inter-
nal or external). You overcome when you do not let either
your emotions or events keep you from being obedient and
faithful.*

If we were given a choice, most of us would choose not
to have obstacles in our path. We would rather have an easy
route to victory. But the sweetest victories are those that involve overcoming—those that involve facing the troubles,
problems, difficulties and challenges and *overcoming* them.

One August morning in 1990 I awakened and immediately
knew that something was wrong. I felt like a Californian who
finally was in "the big one." Ten years earlier I had experi-
enced my first symptoms of MS, and for a decade it had been
creeping into new places in my body. But that morning, as I
struggled to get out of bed, there were some alarming signals
that this was a serious attack. This was a "big one."

Since that morning, I have had to think daily in very specific ways about the whole issue of overcoming. I can no
longer take certain things for granted. I am much more limited in energy. Almost daily, there are a variety of strange,
distracting, sometimes painful or sometimes debilitating symptoms to face. (When I first typed this, I had to stop every few
minutes to let my right arm rest because of weakness and
spasms. Now as I revise this paragraph, my feet are burning
as if on fire, even though I've just come from putting them in
cold water.) I have weeks where I am able to function some-
what normally and then periods where I can do very little
without experiencing extreme fatigue. I will have a good day

and then one where my only option is complete rest. It is not difficult at all to become consumed with the illness.

Mixed in with the challenges of MS for several years were bouts of depression which may or may not have had some medical connection to the MS, depending on which expert one believes. In some ways it was easy for me to write in Part I about "Philip" and in other ways very painful, for I have walked in his shoes.

The encroachment of this illness has changed my life, but one thing has not changed: God still has a plan for me, and that plan involves being a certain kind of person with certain attitudes and traits of character. Furthermore, that plan involves pursuing the mission he has for every Christian's life. As I have faced these facts, it has been absolutely clear to me that to fulfill God's purpose, I must learn to *overcome*. I will overcome these challenges, or they will overcome me.

But I am not alone. My illness has caused me to particularly come to grips with the idea of overcoming, but everyone faces trouble and everyone faces obstacles in their quest to please God. None of us will arrive in heaven because of perfection or achievement, but if we get there, everyone we see who lived to an accountable age on earth will have his or her own story of overcoming. Heaven is for overcomers.

I have known some overcomers in my life. I have known those who have suffered tragedy but kept trusting in God. I have known those who have had debilitating injuries or illnesses but who battled to keep their focus on the good things that God had done for them. I have known Christian women and men whose spouses opposed their faith but who continued faithful without bitterness. I have known others who routinely gave of themselves to the point of weariness, but even then still showed love. I have known those who have sinned grievously, but then faced their sin, turned in a new direction and made great contributions to the kingdom of God. I have known those who faced impossible odds but believed that God's will could still be done, and against the odds, they did it. I am thankful for every example of overcoming and realize that I must give my best to be one of those examples.

Those of us who are disciples of Jesus Christ certainly follow an overcomer. Surely Jesus has our deepest admiration and respect not first of all because he had great natural gifts of leadership and not because he was a teacher of such insight and wisdom. *He is our hero and our role model because he faced hardship, rejection, discouragement, betrayal and violence, and he overcame them.* In spite of those things, he forgave, he loved, he hoped, he rejoiced and he found fulfillment. The Christian gospel is at its heart a story of overcoming—a story of one so determined to help us that he refused to stop until his mission was accomplished. It was not easy. Never ever think it was easy for Jesus. You don't sweat drops of blood over things that are easy. But he is *the* hero because he is the ultimate overcomer.

Now he calls us to be his disciples, and that means he is eager to train *us* to be overcomers. What must you overcome? A background of abuse? The challenge of having a spouse who doesn't share your faith? A serious health problem? A disability? A financial set-back that may affect you for years? Your own past and foolish ventures into sin? An unexplained, but still deep, depression? A persistent character problem you can't seem to change?

I don't know what you have to overcome. But I know you must be an overcomer if you are to be faithful. I don't know if this book will help you to overcome, but I know that if it doesn't, you must find something else that helps you, because one thing is for sure: You *must* be an overcomer.

Chapter Two
Mind Change: The Key to Overcoming

Everything begins in the mind. "As a man thinks. . .so is he" is still true. Many have pointed out that in every situation there are two significant elements: (1) the circumstance itself and (2) the way you think about it. Of the two, however, the second is far more important than the first. As I write this, I am reading a book by a man who was paralyzed in his youth by polio and has had only the use of some toes on one foot throughout most of his forty-plus years, and yet he has earned a college degree and has become an author who types his own manuscripts. His circumstances seem overwhelming, but because of the way he came to think about them, he has been able to overcome.

The point is that overcoming never happens without a "mind change." Overcoming involves facing certain circumstances that would appear to be formidable enough to stop us, but then experiencing a mind change that enables us to push through, climb over, or in some other way, move on to do the will of God.

As I have faced my challenges, I have come to believe that *in every situation there is a right and spiritual way to think that will enable us to overcome whatever challenge we are facing.* In every situation (no matter how difficult it may be), we can experience a mind change from wrong and unspiritual thinking to right and spiritual thinking. It may take some struggle to get to this point, but once the right kind of thinking is at work, we are well on our way to overcoming our circumstances. Consider these passages from Scripture (with emphasis added):

> Those who live according to the sinful nature have their minds set on what that nature desires; but those who live in accordance with the Spirit *have their minds set on what the Spirit desires.* The mind of sinful man is death, but *the mind controlled by the Spirit is life and peace* (Romans 8:5-6).

> Therefore I urge you, brothers, in view of God's mercy, to offer yourselves as living sacrifices, holy and pleasing to God—this is your spiritual act of worship. Do not conform any longer to the pattern of this world, but *be transformed by the renewing of your mind* (Romans 12:1-2a).

> Since, then, you have been raised with Christ, set your hearts on things above where Christ is seated at the right hand of God. *Set your minds on things above,* not on earthly things (Colossians 3:1-2).

> Therefore, *prepare your minds for action*; be self-controlled, set your hope fully on the grace to be given you when Jesus Christ is revealed (1 Peter 1:13).

It is obvious in Scripture that the mind is crucial in finding life, peace and victory.

Author Stephen Covey has popularized the idea of "paradigm shifts." A paradigm shift is simply a new way of looking at something or a new way of thinking about a problem. This is what is involved in overcoming—making paradigm shifts. Shifting from our human and unspiritual way of viewing something to a spiritual and godly way of viewing it. Every time we make that shift and then embrace that new view, we will overcome. It is a spiritual law. God's truth cannot fail. We will reap what we sow. And if we sow a spiritual thought and then persistently cultivate it, we will reap a spiritual victory. "Let us not become weary in doing good, for at the proper time, we will reap a harvest, if we do not give up" (Galatians 6:7-9). Making the right paradigm shifts or the right "mind changes" is the key to overcoming.

Mental Discipline

Such "shifts" will not come about, however, without mental discipline. First, there is the discipline needed to *study* and *grasp* spiritual principles, and then there is the discipline needed to *apply* the right thoughts relentlessly when other unspiritual and unproductive thoughts flow into our minds. We can choose the thoughts that will control our lives, but it takes discipline.

In your house or apartment you have some choices. You have a choice about what color the walls will be. If you decide you want blue walls and you take the time to apply the paint, you don't have to get up each day and decide again that you want the walls to be blue. What you did once will last a long time—assuming you used good paint.

But also, you have a choice about whether you want your house to be neat and clean. This is a choice you do have to remake every day. You can't make a decision on New Year's Day and then automatically get up to a neat, clean house for the next 364 days. No, every day you have to decide again that you want the house to be neat and clean. One thing in particular is required: discipline. Every day you must renew your conviction about keeping order in the house because when there is living going on, there is a natural tendency toward disorder.

Choosing our thoughts is much more like the second situation. You may wish that you could choose to see everything spiritually and never have to give it a second thought, but it hardly works that way. You can choose what thoughts you will have. You can choose what thoughts will dominate your mind, but you will have to exercise a great deal of mental discipline. Some of us, because of our tendencies, will have to exercise even more discipline than others. But for all of us, such mental discipline will be the key to overcoming.

One of our daughters recently received a new point-and-shoot camera as a gift. As we read the instructions, we learned to look through the viewfinder at the object and press the shutter halfway down. This causes a green light in the viewfinder to blink. The shutter is to be held in that position until the green light stops blinking and becomes a constant. This indicates that the focus is now properly locked on the object to be photographed. Overcoming involves getting spiritual truth in front of our eyes and staying with it until our focus is locked on it. Sometimes, as with the camera, that takes only a moment. Sometimes it takes much longer. What is needed is the mental discipline to persevere until we are locked into God's view of a situation.

While there will be many circumstances we cannot change, we can always change our minds, and that will change the outcome.

Chapter Three
But. . .God

Consider one very important example of how we must discipline our thinking. Many of us are aware of God's promises and clearly stated spiritual laws. Let's call these the "positives." We are also aware of the problems, challenges and difficulties that life presents to us. Let's call these the "negatives." Our failure comes in the way we put these things together.

In years of counseling and working with others, here is the kind of thing I have heard over and over:

> "I know God says he will meet all our needs, *but* there are so many needs in my life that I just don't see how it is going to happen."

> "I know God says we are to be making disciples, *but* my circumstances right now are so difficult and my life is so stressful."

> "The Bible says God works for our good in everything, *but* I can't see any good at all in what's happening to me."

> "I know the Bible teaches that we will not be tempted beyond what we can bear, *but* I am so weak and the temptation is so strong."

Not only have I heard these things from others over and over, but I have said things like this when being counseled myself or when wrestling with some challenging issue. But do you see the common element in this kind of thinking? Simply diagrammed it is this:

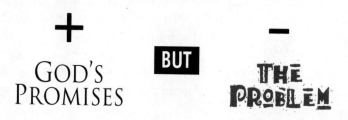

The pattern in our thinking is (1) to acknowledge what God has said and, therefore, what is right and what is true and then (2) to throw in that crucial word "but" and finally (3) to tack on the negative circumstances. Whenever we use the word "but" in a sentence or in our thoughts, we go away emphasizing and focusing on whatever comes after the word "but," not what comes before it.

To be even more specific, the way we are thinking may look more like this:

We see God somewhere in the picture, but in our minds the problem looks so much bigger than God.

Overcoming involves a mind change. It involves taking all the same pieces of information but disciplining ourselves to think of them in a different way, so our new thinking looks like this:

Or, as in the second case, a change would look something like this, as we stand more in awe of God than we do of our problem:

Such a mind change does not mean we push anything under the rug. On the left side we can lay it all out and describe in great detail just how miserable or difficult the situation is. We can paint it with bold and vivid colors. David does this in many of his Psalms. Consider these lines from Psalm 6 and Psalm 13:

> My soul is in anguish.
> How long, O Lord, how long?

> . . . I am worn out from groaning;
>   all night long I flood my bed with weeping
>   and drench my couch with tears.
> My eyes grow weak with sorrow. . .
>   (Psalm 6:3, 6-7).

> How long, O Lord? Will you forget me
>   forever?
>   How long will you hide your face from me?
> How long must I wrestle with my thoughts
>   and have sorrow in my heart?
>   How long must my enemy triumph over me?
>   (Psalm 13:1-2).

But once all the pain and problems have been described, then we must add that all-important word "but" and then God's powerful promises and vital truth. If you keep reading in these Psalms you will see that this is exactly what David did (emphasis added):

> *[But]* The Lord has heard my cry for mercy.
>   The Lord accepts my prayer.
> All my enemies will be ashamed and dismayed
>   (Psalm 6:9-10).

> *But* I trust in your unfailing love; my heart
>   rejoices in your salvation.
> I will sing to the Lord
>   for he has been good to me (Psalm 13:5).

Not only do we see this pattern so clearly in the Psalms, but it comes through in passages like 2 Corinthians 1 and 4. Listen to the way Paul talks about his own challenges (emphasis added):

> We were under great pressure, far beyond our ability to endure, so that we despaired even of life. Indeed in our heart we felt the very sentence of death. *But* this happened so that we might not rely on ourselves but on God who raises the dead (2 Corinthians 1: 8b-9).

> But we have this treasure in jars of clay to show that this all-surpassing power is from God and not from us. We are hard pressed on every side, *but* not crushed; perplexed; *but* not in despair; persecuted *but* not abandoned; struck down *but* not destroyed (2 Corinthians 4:7-9).

When this approach is applied to the kind of situations mentioned earlier, here is what we come up with:

> "There are so many needs in my life, and I can't see how it is all going to work out, *but* I know God has promised to meet every need and he is always faithful."

> "My circumstances are very challenging and there is a lot that could be getting me down, *but* God has called us to make disciples in all circumstances, and he can enable me to do that and bless me with fruitfulness, even with all that is going on."

"Right now things are tough, and I admit I get confused sometimes about what God is trying to show me or do with me, *but* he promised that he would work for good in all things, and I am holding on to that promise."

"I feel very weak, and the temptations often look like giants in my life, *but* God has promised that he will not allow us to be tempted beyond what we can bear, and my situation is not a strange exception to that. With God's help, I can be another David who slays the giants."

Such a mind change is amazingly simple, but one that many of us can make only as we seriously discipline our thinking. We so naturally think "positive, but negative." It is deep in our hearts, and it comes so quickly out of our mouths. We must start by recognizing how biblical and right (and powerful) the "negative, but positive" pattern is. Humble yourself and cry out to God for the discipline to change your pattern. Your first efforts may sound something like this:

"God, it is so easy for me to quote your promises and turn around and discount them with the negatives of life, *but* with your help I can begin to think the way you want to me to think. And furthermore, God, I will not stop until I make this change. It may be tough, *but* you are powerful and can help even me to change. It may take a lot of work, *but* the changes you want are always worth it."

For many of us, the natural tendency is to say, "but...problems" or "but...obstacles." To be overcomers we must experience a mind change and learn to say simply, "Yes...problems, yes...obstacles, but God!" If it takes a lot of mental discipline to get to this point and stay at this point, so be it. There is no other way to be an overcomer.

Chapter Four
Faith and Prayer

Scripture teaches "this is the victory that overcomes the world, even our faith" (1 John 5:4). Ultimately, there will be no overcomers who are not people of faith. Ultimately, your faith in God and in his power will be the key to every effort that overcomes. But without mental discipline, something other than faith will dominate your thoughts. Without mental discipline, faith cannot replace worry, anxiety, fear or selfishness. That's probably why Peter says, "Therefore be clear minded and self-controlled so that you can pray" (1 Peter 4:7). Faith is the beginning and the end of the matter. At the beginning, you want to overcome and do the will of God because of your faith. In the end, overcoming will always involve holding on to your faith through thick and thin. But in the middle will be the mental discipline that rejects whatever is not consistent with faith and holds on to whatever faith is teaching you.

At the beginning must be a decision that nothing is more important than maintaining faith and following wherever it leads. In the middle must be a mental toughness that refuses to let go of faith regardless of what beats on it. Where there is that kind of beginning and that kind of middle, there will be an end where faith overcomes.

Ultimately, faith is the victory that overcomes, not because of some inherent power in faith but because of the object of faith. To say "I know this is true, but God is greater" is to put your confidence in God. Faith is involved in overcoming because faith is what connects us to God and releases his power within us. We can never boast about overcoming, for anytime we overcome and do what pleases God, it will be God who deserves the credit and God who should get the glory. We need mental discipline, but watch out for the thought, *I overcame because of my mental discipline.* In such a situation, we may have won a battle but lost the war. We may have won a battle over some circumstance, but we will have lost the larger spiritual war against pride and self-sufficiency. We may have overcome something, but something else much larger and more deadly will have overcome us.

While getting our minds properly focused is essential for effective prayer (see 1 Peter 4:7 above), we must also recognize the role prayer plays in helping us properly focus our minds. The two elements cannot be dissociated from one another, and it is not possible to say with certainty which one comes first.

There are days when we must walk with God (or fall before God) and say, "Help me, Father, get my mind where it needs to be. Wrong thoughts are coming from everywhere. The battle is intense. Help me think your thoughts. Help me see life the way you see it. Give me clear vision and proper perspective."

Because I have MS most of you could easily pull something away from me that I might be holding in my hands. As much as I might want to keep it, my strength would not be enough for me to win a tug-a-war with you. In the same way, there are days when I take out truth from God and read it, but powerful circumstances and forces are trying to pull it from me. At such times I must pray for God to put it on my heart and fix it in my mind. Only as I persist in prayer do I find the mental strength needed to hold on.

No Christian should ever think there will be true over-coming without prayer. I have prayed that nothing in this book will lead you to think that victory is found through your own "positive thinking." As you get to the "power thoughts" at the back of this book, keep in mind that they are not meant to be used without prayer. Those who benefit from them will be those who *pray their way through them*. While I am trying to rightly emphasize how powerful our thoughts are and how we must take the responsibility for controlling them, I know our thinking will ultimately fail us if it is not focused on God and drawing us to him. If the mind change brought about does not result in people on their knees be-fore God seeking strength and power from him, our victories will be temporary at best.

In a future book, I hope we can explore more fully the power released in prayer, for it deserves much more atten-tion, but let me say that nothing you are reading here would have been written without prayer. I have no doubt about it: Apart from prayer, I would not be an overcomer, and I cer-tainly wouldn't be writing a book about it. Jesus clearly be-lieved with all his being that he could not overcome without the power he found in his relationship with God (John 5:19, 30). No wonder he often withdrew to private places and prayed

(Luke 5:16). No wonder he sometimes went out to pray and felt such need for it that he prayed all night (Luke 6:12). His actions speak. He was convinced he would not overcome without prayer—constant, fervent, persistent prayer. Do you share his conviction?

David's mind change described earlier, which left him focused on God and not his pain, was worked out in prayer. The Psalms we referenced—Psalm 6 and 13—were prayers. The very best way to switch our thinking is to do it in prayer, for in communion with God we find resources outside ourselves to take us places we could never go relying on ourselves.

What would happen if your prayer life changed dramatically? What if you prayed more consistently with more confidence? What if prayer changed from being a significant piece of your life to the very center of your life?

Would you be less or more likely to overcome your challenge? Would you be less likely to overcome a besetting sin or more likely? Would you be less likely or more likely to stay joyful, even through some very tough times? Would you be less likely or more likely to see God demonstrate his power, even in your weakness? Prayer can make a remarkable difference. Thinking rightly about it is a part of the needed mind change, but then as God comes to us through prayer, we will make even more mind changes which will ensure victory.

For those of you who like summaries and outlines, here is what we have looked at so far:

1. We are in the world to do the will of God.
2. There are powerful opponents and obstacles.
3. We do not have in ourselves what it takes to overcome.
4. God has graciously provided everything we need. He has revealed the truth that can transform our lives.
5. He tells us it will take renewing and disciplining our minds to overcome.
6. If we will seek, we will find. If we will ask, God will give. We can seek the mental discipline needed, and we can find it.
7. Through consistent prayer, God will help us lock our focus on to spiritual truths.
8. With prayer, we can put those spiritual truths into practice and God will work powerfully.
9. When we live in such a way, we will be overcomers because our lives will please God whatever the circumstances.
10. To God goes all the glory, because without his truth and his help we would have never overcome.

Chapter Five
The Principle Applied: Overcoming Discouragement

As we think about overcoming, I want to address one particularly stubborn problem—discouragement. Some people by temperament are more easily discouraged than others, but almost all of us have to deal with it at one time or another. Remember our basic thesis: *In every situation there is a right and spiritual way to think that will enable us to overcome whatever challenge we are facing. In every situation we can experience a mind change from wrong and unspiritual thinking to right and spiritual thinking.* When we fall into discouragement, we must shift from seeing it as a valid experience which must be allowed to run its murky course to seeing it as an alien force that must be dealt with decisively.

When a person is in the state of discouragement, his mind is usually working something like this:

> *I tried hard. I did what I thought one was supposed to do. But what did it get me? The result I worked for and prayed for did not come. I'm discouraged AND I HAVE A RIGHT TO FEEL THIS WAY!*

That last phrase is the key one. When we are discouraged, we believe we have a right to feel this way. Our natural minds tell us that we have been wronged, and we have a right to feel wronged. I don't think I have ever talked with a discouraged person who didn't in some way believe that he or she had a right to that feeling. That's why they held on to it so stubbornly.

Some years ago, I came upon a new approach to working with MS. This medical and nutritional regime was a tough one, but after much prayer, I committed myself to it. However, after several months on the program, I noticed little change. Naturally, I felt I deserved better. I was working hard at this thing, but seeming to get little from it. "Don't be discouraged," said the doctor. "It takes time." But I wasn't seeing the results I wanted and feelings of discouragement came, particularly as I considered how much sacrifice I was making to be consistent with this program. My mind told me it was only natural to feel this way and that I had a right to my feelings.

At various times in my life as a disciple, I have done what disciples are supposed to do, but have not seen the results I wanted to see. I have poured myself out for people in my effort to help them get to God. I have expended time and effort for them, but they have not always responded. At such times, feelings of discouragement often showed up. Not surprisingly, the more I had invested, the more discouragement I felt. Put in much, get back little. It seemed I had a right to be down.

But if we are going to overcome, we must deal with discouragement, and dealing with it starts with seeing it accurately. When we are in a state of discouragement, we have taken our eyes off of God and off of the goal, and we have put our eyes on our effort, our pain and our wounds. Discouragement has two big brothers—self-pity and self-righteousness—and sometimes they both show up. The first we probably expected. The second surprises us. Self-pity says, "Poor me. Things just don't work out for me like they do for some people, so I have a right to be down." Self-righteousness says, "I deserve better than this, since I did what was right and put out such an effort. At least I should get to wear my purple heart of discouragement. I earned it." Self-pity and self-righteousness are convincing fellows and strong defenders of their little brother, but unless we deal with this odious trio, we have no chance of being overcomers. Listen to them, defend their cause and you will become an unmotivated, self-centered little wimp, and even your mother won't enjoy being around you.

There is a difference between knee-jerk feelings of disappointment and a decision we make to let those disappointments put us in a state of discouragement. There is a difference between (1) answering the door to find discouragement standing there starting his sales pitch and (2) inviting him in to fill up your home with his dour message. I have not found a way to keep discouragement from ever showing up, but I have found that when he appears, God can always give us a mind change that makes it possible for us to shut the door on "Mr. D" and send him back out in the cold.

Here are examples of how this can work:

"I am disappointed. I prayed a lot about this person. I served him and gave him my heart, and still he didn't respond to the message. *But* it is right to give even when we get nothing in return. God has done a lot of giving to those who haven't responded. Yes, I'm disappointed. Yes, it hurts. *But* it is like God to give, and if I keep giving, there will be a harvest. God has promised it."

"I am feeling discouraged and unmotivated. I've prayed about my health and nothing seems to change. I've tried different things, and each time I think (or hope) I've found an answer, I'm disappointed. I'm struggling big time with self-pity. *But* I can't stay in these feelings. A better man than I am also cried out to God because he wanted to get better, and here's the answer he got: 'My grace is sufficient for you. My power is made perfect in weakness.' If God chooses to leave some of these problems in my life, he can work through them. He even says he can make his power *perfect* in them."

"Not only am I down, but I'm thinking I have a right to be here. Something tells me we don't expect an injured person to be jumping hurdles, so why should we expect a person who has taken the hits from life to be enthusiastic about anything? *But* what am I thinking? Did God ever promise me a life with no pain? Did Jesus ever say, 'In this world you will not have trouble?' Everyone in the world goes through pain. Do I think I'm so different that I should not have to? Have I forgotten that the only really good man went through the worst pain? Have I forgotten that at the heart of my faith is a God who worked through pain?"

Do you get the idea? Talk to yourself. Admit those natural feelings, but then respond to them. Execute a mind change. Go ahead, lay out the pain, but end with faith! The Psalmist did:

> These things I remember as I pour out my soul:
> how I used to go with the multitude,
> leading the procession to the house of God,
> with shouts of joy and thanksgiving among the
> festive throng.
> Why are you downcast, O my soul?
> Why so disturbed within me?
> Put your hope in God, for I will yet praise him,
> my Savior and my God (Psalm 42:4-6a).

Here is the truth: It is never God's will for us to live in a state of discouragement. It is even more wrong for us to defend our right to be there. Fight it. Don't defend it. Oswald Chambers says some things go more by kicking than by praying. Discouragement may be one of those things, but probably the best answer is to pray while you kick. But whatever you do, don't let it settle in and don't let it win. Get your eyes back on your goal and back on your God. Discipline your mind, let the word of Christ dwell in you richly so you can teach and admonish yourself with all wisdom. Do it first to yourself, and then you will have the conviction and the credibility to help others.

> The Lord himself goes before you and will be with you; he will never leave you nor forsake you. Do not be afraid; do not be discouraged (Deuteronomy 31:8).

Chapter Six
Life

In the next three chapters, I want to challenge you to change your mind about life, about God and about your circumstances. I want to let you know how my thinking was wrong in these areas and how I have found new power in changing my mind.

Many of us, particularly those of us who are Americans, have been taught to think that life is supposed to be easy. The government refers to some of the country's social programs as "entitlements" and that word describes exactly what many of us feel. We feel *entitled* to a certain kind of life, certain comforts and certain freedoms. Then when things don't go our way, we can get a real attitude—a real bad attitude!

As Americans, we live in the country that believes in life, liberty and the pursuit of happiness, and when something comes along that messes up our happiness, we ask the big questions. And they're not "What can I learn from this?" or "What new perspective is this giving me?" The big questions are "Why me?" "What did I do to deserve this?" "Why is this happening to me now, just when everything seemed to be going right for a change?"

The way we react when hard times come reveals so much about who we are and what we really believe. We think we have some unalienable right for life to always work out the way we want it to or least 80 or 90 percent of the time. And then when it doesn't, we are ready to throw a pity party with black and gray balloons, or we are quick to get a good lawyer, fight back and get what we deserve.

My wife's favorite movie, *Lost in Yonkers*, is one most people didn't get that excited about. (She just has better taste than most!) The main character, played by Mercedes Rule, is Belle, a woman in her mid-thirties living in New York in the 1940s. Belle has a very childlike personality and is a bit on the slow side. After meeting a guy who wants to marry her, she decides to get her family (mother, aunt, brother and nephews) together to announce the big news. After dinner she begins to seat everyone in the parlor just where she wants them to be. All of this is driving her brother, played by Richard Dryfuss, absolutely crazy. He keeps pacing around the room, refusing to sit down. Belle pleads with him to come over and sit in his designated spot, but he refuses. Finally, in desperation she cries out, "No, no! You can't sit there. This is not the way I pictured it."

This line has become a favorite around our house. If I have plans for a romantic evening and have trouble getting my wife on my wave length, I say, "Honey, this is not the way I pictured it." We both have a good laugh, and then we get on with my agenda!

But seriously, the truth is that this is the way a lot of us are about life. We get attitudes toward other people or we get attitudes toward God because things aren't working out "the way I pictured it." We practically canonize our own expectations and treat them as the *67th* book of the Bible. We somehow think God has the responsibility to make it all work out just as we pictured it.

What we have to do is change our minds about life. *Life was not our idea.* We did not create it. We did not create the world, and we did not create ourselves. We simply do not have some unalienable right to have it our way. This makes a lot of sense if you stop and think about it, but for most people this represents a huge change in thinking.

Now you may not think you're a "have it my way" person, but watch your reactions when things don't go as you pictured them. For example, you're in pretty good shape. You do the things that are supposed to help people stay healthy and strong and energetic, but then you get terribly sick. Do you think: "This doesn't seem fair. I did all the right things. There is some mistake; this is wrong." Do you grumble and complain? If you do, it's because you think you have some sort of right to have life always work out according to your plans.

We need to change our minds about life. Life is a gift. It comes from someone else, and it comes to accomplish his purposes, *not ours.* When you change your mind about this, it changes the way you look at a lot of things.

I think about two biblical passages. The first is John 6:38:

"For I have come down from heaven not to do my will but to do the will of him who sent me."

Jesus understood life and thought correctly about it. He understood that while on this earth he was not here to please himself, fulfill himself, get what he wanted, have all his dreams come true, or to have it be just the way he pictured it, but he was here *to do the will of him who sent him*. And so when Satan hit him with tough temptations, he didn't say, "This isn't fair." When the people rejected him, he didn't say, "This isn't the way I pictured it." And when they marched him toward crucifixion, he didn't call down twelve legions of angels to stop the insanity. Even his cry from the cross, "My God, my God why have you forsaken me?" was not the moment when he finally turned selfish, but instead it was both a fulfillment of Psalm 22 and a statement of how far the Suffering Servant would go to save us from our sin.

We need to change our minds about life and see it the way Jesus did. We must see that we are not here to have the pleasure we want or to avoid the pain we don't want, but we are here to do the will of God—whatever that may be.

I first wrote this chapter on a day when a major snow storm hit New England. Our youngest daughter, home from school, had just returned from the mailbox. Mixed in with all the Christmas cards from friends and relatives was a touching note from a woman in Toronto. My daughter met her during the summer when the woman was joyfully carrying her first child. But the note reported that the child was stillborn in November—certainly far from the way she and her husband had dreamed it would be. But they are disciples, and they understand what Jesus was talking about. Sure, they felt pain and grief, but they are accepting this event as a part of a much bigger picture. Her card was most encouraging to my daughter even with what they had been through.

There will always be some tough times, but thank God that as we do his will, we will also have much joy and a lot of good old-fashioned fun; we will find life to the full. But we are not here to demand that it work out on our terms. We are here to do what my friend Gordon Ferguson describes in his powerful book *The Victory of Surrender*—we are here to surrender to God and God's purposes.*

In the "Power Thoughts" section of this book, I include a quote of Amy Carmichael that is one of my favorites: "We are not here to wish to be somewhere or something we are not, but to do the thing that pleases him, exactly where we are and as we are." That is the way Jesus looked at it, and that is the way we need to look at it. When we stop and think about life in this way, it is liberating.

I had to change my mind about life. I looked at MS, and thought,

> *I don't like this. I don't want this. This isn't fair. I need to keep a full schedule. I can't afford to have to take these two- and three-hour naps. God has given me more than twenty-five years of valuable spiritual experience. The church needs people like me to be active and involved. Beyond that, I need to be able to play golf and tennis. I need these things for my sanity. I need them to build relationships. God, this isn't the way I pictured it.*

But I've had to change my mind and say, "This is God's life not mine. He owns it, I don't. I don't have some right for A, B, C and D to all work out just as I planned. When I've

*Gordon Ferguson, *Victory of Surrender* (Woburn, Mass.: Discipleship Publications International, 1995).

surrendered to God's plan, can you guess what has happened? Just what he promised: I have found life (and have just recently been able to get back on the golf course once in a while with a little help from an electric cart!).

The second passage that helps me change my thoughts about life is James 4:13-15:

> Now listen, you who say, "Today or tomorrow we will go to this or that city, spend a year there, carry on business and make money." Why, you do not even know what will happen tomorrow. What is your life? You are a mist that appears for a little while and then vanishes. Instead, you ought to say, "If it is the Lord's will, we will live and do this or that."

The first attitude described in this passage assumes that life is fundamentally ours and should be under our control. The second attitude represents a mind change that says, "No, life is God's, and if it's his will, we will do this and that." When you have the second attitude—the right one—then changes or challenges do not get you wrapped around the axle, because you know there is a larger plan and God is still in control.

Changing my mind about life involves changing my mind about God, and that is what we will examine more closely in the next chapter.

Chapter Seven
God

Some of us have a rather strange God. He is big enough to create the world and a universe with billions of stars. He has enough power and savvy to use his church to take the gospel around the world. But oddly, he is not big enough to take care of our common problems. So we have to carry them around all by ourselves until our spiritual spines are so bent that the best chiropractor could not help us.

We have a God who is able to rip apart the Iron Curtain, tear down the Berlin Wall and bring the Gospel to places where no one had heard it for years. He can rearrange the political landscape and open dozens of new doors. He can bring together in one body all kinds of natural and historic enemies. Many reading this book have seen nothing short of miracles in his church at the end of the twentieth century. But sometimes we have a schizophrenic faith. We are not sure he can take care of *us*.

When we capture the thoughts going through our heads, we find things like: *I wonder what is going to happen to me. Has God forgotten me? Are others going to have a useful life while I'm left on the outside?*

Circumstances mess with our emotions, and then our emotions mess with our minds, and we end up thinking that somehow the great God of the Cosmos is stumped by our problems. We have a God who can move mountains, but is at a loss to know what to do with someone who is paralyzed or someone with cancer or someone with MS or someone with one of those diseases that is very real but seemingly undiagnosable. We have a God who could deliver Israel from Pharaoh, but cannot deliver us from our financial situation or the deep sense of loss we feel or the darkness of depression.

We need to change our minds about God. He is not made in our image so that he is sometimes strong and sometimes weak. He is not a God who has good days and bad days. He came in Jesus and lived among us, but he did not pick up our bad habits. He is not the God who can move big projects, but cannot help little people.

After the first edition of this book was released, someone told me that one of his favorites passages in the Power Thoughts section is "Today, tomorrow, forever, God is God. He is never surprised or unprepared. He never asks, 'What are we going to do now?'"

But some of us act like God cannot figure us out and cannot figure out our situation. We embellish the seriousness of our problems and act like God is just avoiding us because he doesn't want to admit that he doesn't have any answers either. Our God is the popular god of modern theology who cares but is powerless to meet our needs.

I was once in that boat, but one of my closest friends helped me to think differently. Gordon Ferguson will tell you that he could not totally figure me out, but he kept telling me that God could. And God did.

I have to put into practice what I wrote about in Chapter 3. I have to say, "But...God," and then I have to let the God in that statement really be God. I have to say, Yes, I have MS. Yes, the stiffness in my legs is ferocious. Yes, the normal medication for that problem does not help me even at high dosages. Yes, my fatigue seems to be getting worse. Yes, I have to miss a lot of meetings and fun activities. *But...God.* God is not intimidated by my MS. It does not in any way threaten the plan he has for my life. It does not keep him from getting *anything* done with me that *he* wants to get done. What an amazing thought! *Lord, help me hold on to it.*

Do I wake up thinking these thoughts every morning? No, I have already said that what is in my mind when I wake up is not always pretty, but that's why I have quiet times—to change my mind. To get my mind back on to the truth.

I have given you an example from my life, but you must apply it to your own situation. A lot of us have a lot of wrong ideas about God. We have allowed our interpretation of circumstances and the resulting emotions to cause us to think a lot of wrong things.

- We think he doesn't care.
- We think he is vindictive and holds grudges.
- We think that some problems, as big as they are to us, are too small for his intervention.
- We think he can't relate to what we are going through.

All of these are wrong ideas, and they can all be challenged and corrected. Whatever thought keeps us from being confident that God is present, concerned and capable, it needs to change and it can change.

The key to right living is right thinking about God. If you have wrong thoughts about God and you don't challenge them and change them, you will not be an overcomer. You will be overcome.

The day I wrote this chapter, I woke up about at 5:00 A.M. in a flood of negative thoughts—a mixture of guilt, anxiety, dread and anger. While I can't really tell you why, because I don't exactly know, I can tell you what I did about it. I took about forty-five minutes just thinking about the character of God. I described him to myself in great detail from what the Scriptures teach. I meditated on his qualities one by one and prayed about each one.

By the time my wife awoke, I was eager to pray with her. I thanked God for how much he has revealed to us about his nature, character and power. Bringing the real God right into the middle of my world had made me very grateful and confident it was not going to be a bad day after all, and it has not been!

I am convinced that a crucial key to overcoming is spending time with God that is

- daily
- personal
- characterized by a total surrender to his purposes.

Get this kind of time every day, and you will be on your way to right thinking about God and on your way to victory.

Chapter Eight
Circumstances

Most of the time people see their circumstances as problems, as barriers, as obstacles—even as excuses. We must change our minds about circumstances. We must look at life through a spiritual lens and see that every circumstance is not as much a problem as it is an opportunity. Few stories in the Bible illustrate this better than John 9:1-3:

> As he [Jesus] went along, he saw a man blind from birth. His disciples asked him, "Rabbi, who sinned, this man or his parents, that he was born blind?"
> "Neither this man nor his parents sinned," said Jesus, "but this happened so that the work of God might be displayed in his life."

The disciples needed a mind change. They saw a man with an optical challenge. Jesus saw a challenging opportunity—an opportunity for God to show his power.

We need to change our minds about pain, about weakness, about fatigue, about rejection, and we need to see that every one of these is an opportunity for God to work.

"But I would rather him work some other way," you say. Well, the problem is not your circumstances. It is what Gordon Ferguson calls your own God-playing little heart. Spiritual success does not come to those who want to call the

shots and have God rubber-stamp their decisions. In 2 Corinthians 12, the overcomer's golden text, we learn that Paul, too,
wanted God to work some other way. He desperately wanted
him to take away that thorn in his flesh. He no doubt thought
that his work absolutely required that it be removed. But God
stunned him by saying in essence, "No. This is an opportunity,
Paul, for me to show how powerful I am—an opportunity to
show how much I can work through weakness."

Some months ago I had the opportunity to make my first
trip to Africa. (Since my most severe MS attack, I have traveled to three continents where I had never been before. In-
teresting how God works.) While in Johannesburg, I was first
able to hear a leader from the church in Lagos, Nigeria, speak
and later have some time to talk with him and his wife. If you
think your circumstances are challenging, I would encourage
you to consider theirs.

Oneychi Oguaha and his wife, Desi, simply expect life in
that city of ten million to be hard, even disastrous. They expect that the power will go off several times during the day.
They expect that when they are meeting as a church the
lights will go off and the microphone will go dead. They
don't expect the phone system to work. They expect the garbage to pile up in the streets. They expect political turmoil.
They expect violence. They expect that there will be no gaso-
line and that the disciples and their visitors will often have to
walk miles to get to church. They expect that rains will turn
many of the roads into mud.

Oneychi described how in the previous year, he and his
family had malaria three times. Sometimes he and Desi had

to stay up all night fanning their children who had high fevers. Both he and his wife had typhoid, which is acquired only through drinking water that has been contaminated with sewage. Twenty percent of the church had typhoid during that year.

Some of us would look at these circumstances and see nothing but problems; I am afraid I would be counted among them. Nechi and Desi see opportunities. They see an opportunity to show a country and a city something it has never seen—a way to be joyful and thankful in the midst of overwhelming difficulties. They see an opportunity to introduce people to the living God who is greater than all these challenges. Oneychi described one Sunday morning when 1500 disciples were waving little Nigerian flags and saying with that gesture, "We are thankful to be here and we are not leaving." In a country where most people say, "I hate Nigeria and desperately want to get out," this is a powerful statement. No wonder God is blessing their vision and their faith. No wonder the church is exploding with growth.

After I heard Oneychi speak, I was sitting quietly thinking about the whole new paradigm he had given me for my life, when someone came over and said to me, "I want to thank you for your book *Mind Change.*" It was the first time I can remember not appreciating a compliment. It seemed out of place. Without a moment's hesitation I pointed toward Oneychi and said, "There is the man who should have written the book." Yes, I still have MS with all the challenge that it brings, but my brothers and sisters in Nigeria gave me a whole new way of looking at everything. I knew at that moment I would never be the same. Even as I write this, I look over my shoulder at a little Nigerian flag that hangs in my office at home as a reminder many months later of the lessons learned that day.

I don't always like my circumstances. But I am learning that God would not allow them if they were not opportunities for me to do something more important than I would have been doing without them. What looks to me like something that is hindering the work of God (like Paul's thorn in the flesh) is often a vehicle God plans to use for one of his patented surprise attacks. Change your mind about circumstances.

Don't think:	**Think:**
• "This is terrible."	• "This is terribly important."
• "This is awful."	• "This is an awfully interesting challenge."
• "Why did God allow this bad thing?"	• "What is God going to do through this bad thing?"

You may read what I have written and say: "But my mind doesn't change easily." My question for you is how much do you want to be an overcomer? How persistent are you willing to be? You may say, "My problem is that I change my mind, but then it changes back. I can't get it to stay put on the right things." I can relate to that one. Several years ago I told several friends that I must have a Teflon mind because nothing seemed to stick to it. But you see, even that very circumstance is allowed by God. Circumstances will reveal how much you want to find God's thinking and how persistent you are willing to be to hold on to it.

My message in these three chapters is this: Don't allow yourself to be tossed to and fro by whatever comes along. Examine your thoughts. Test them. Scrutinize them. And then change them when they need to be changed. Change them so that line up with the truth—the truth about life, the truth about God and the truth about circumstances. You will find once again that when you know the truth, the truth will set you free.

Chapter Nine
Two Minds Are Better Than One

Each of us must take responsibility for our own lives. We must not think of ourselves as victims of events, circumstances and problems. We must understand that in any situation, we can change our minds and begin to think spiritually, correctly and even powerfully. We must not blame our failures or ineffectiveness on someone else's failure to give us what we thought we needed from them. Blaming where you are in your life on anything or anyone else is a sure road to repeated failure. Overcomers don't have "blaming" in their arsenal.

But having stressed our personal responsibility, we must also stress the biblical concept of the body of Christ. We are not fighting our battles alone. We are not running this race by ourselves. God has given us other people to help us get our minds where they need to be and to overcome our challenges.

> Just as each of us has one body with many members, and these members do not all have the same function, so in Christ we who are many form one body, and each member belongs to all the others (Romans 12:4-5).

> If one part suffers, every part suffers with it; if one part is honored, every part rejoices with it. Now you are the body of Christ and each one of you is part of it (1 Corinthians 12:26-27).

We have been brought together to be there for one another. It is clear that in these relationships we are to be bringing truth to each other—helping each other stay focused on those things which will lead to victory.

> Let the word of Christ dwell in you richly as you teach and admonish one another with all wisdom. . . (Colossians 3:16).

> Therefore encourage one another with these words (1 Thessalonians 4:18).

> But encourage one another daily, as long as it is called Today, so that none of you may be hardened by sin's deceitfulness (Hebrews 3:13).

As we change our paradigm and look at our lives, problems, difficulties and challenges through God's eyes, one of the things we will see is how he has put other people in our lives to help us. I believe that if I were to get totally isolated from others through no choice of my own (let's say in solitary confinement in a POW camp), God would stand by me and give me all the strength I needed (as he did Paul in a similar situation described in 2 Timothy 4:17). But that is not normally our situation. Most of us can choose to be in the fellowship, living our lives in the presence of and with the help of others. God will still work in the extraordinary circumstances of isolation, but that is not how he plans for us normally to be overcomers, and that is never a situation we should choose.

You and I need convictions. We need convictions that we hold to whether someone is encouraging our faithfulness or not. But at the same time, recognizing the weakness in our own flesh and the enormous power of our enemy, we must seek out all the help God makes available to us. The person who says, "I'm going to be an overcomer, and I'm going to do it all by myself" doesn't have a biblical attitude, and he or she won't get a biblical victory.

Whatever you face, you will need the "but...God" mindset that we described earlier, but that doesn't mean you should stoically stuff feelings about past hurts, present conflicts or emotions you do not totally understand. If these are present, you will need help working them through. You will also need counsel to evaluate new challenges and figure out just what "but...God" means, given new developments.

In my case, I have been applying the principles I am writing about here for some time. I have worked on disciplining my mind and keeping it focused on God's truth. The results have been powerful. But I still very much need other people. There are times when a new flurry of MS symptoms hits or the normal fatigue from the disease just wears me down or something tough happens completely unrelated to my illness, and I need another person to use his or her mind to help my mind stay on track. I need encouragement, reminders and challenges. I need people who are more objective about me than I am. I need people who can help me see my blind spots. Haven't you noticed? Two minds are better than one.

Of course, when the Bible calls us into relationship with one another, it is not just to help each other with problem solving, to give each other reminders or to keep each other on the correct track. We are called into relationships to love one another—to build family, to make each other feel appreciated, needed and special. In such an atmosphere, it is so much easier to hold tightly to truth. Writing about his relationship with the disciples in Colosse, Paul said,

> My purpose is that they may be encouraged in heart and united in love, so that they may have the full riches of complete understanding, in order that they may know the mystery of God, namely, Christ. . . (Colossians 2:2).

When we are united in love with others and *experience it emotionally,* our hearts will be more encouraged and our minds much more receptive to right ways of thinking.

We were made for love and all our efforts to overcome will be amazingly strengthened by love.

Some years ago, as I struggled with my illness and battled with a tenacious depression, I had some very mature and wise people in my life who could not figure me out. They wanted to have the answers. They wanted to find out how to fix me, but they will tell you today that they were perplexed. But in spite of their frustration and limitations, they did the right thing: *They kept loving me.* And, fortunately, I did the right thing: *I let them.* Looking back, I know they said things that helped. They gave me insights that were useful. But nothing was more important than the fact that they made me feel respected, appreciated and valuable when I had a hard time believing any of those things were true. Their love kept me in the race until my mind finally became capable of locking onto the truth.

So keep your balance. Take responsibility for your own life. Realize you hold the key to what will happen to you. Develop your own faith, your own convictions and your own walk with God. Never blame anyone else for what is happening to you. At the same time, don't try to be the Lone Ranger or the solitary warrior. Look at life through the mind of Christ, and see how he bought with his blood a fellowship in which we will both get help and give it to others. Be honest enough to tell others where you need help. Be humble enough to receive the help. Always make it your goal to give as much as you get and pass on to others the help you yourself have received from God (2 Corinthians 1). This is a sure formula for overcoming.

Chapter Ten
When We Sin

We are sinners. We are sinners loved by God. In Christ, we are sinners redeemed by his blood. We are sinners who are saved and sinners who have hope. *But we are still sinners.* The Bible is perfectly clear about this. The most mature disciple you know, the one you rightly respect and imitate, is still a sinner. All long-term efforts to overcome will be checkered with sin and with failures. Overcoming must involve facing this fact and finding biblical solutions.

As you tackle your most challenging circumstances with the kind of faith and thinking we have described briefly in this book, you will still sin. It is much better not to sin. Like the apostle John, we are writing these things so that you will not sin. But, also like John, we recognize that along the line somewhere, you will (1 John 2:1-2). What you do when this happens is most critical to your efforts to be an overcomer.

Let me use myself as an example. As I work with my illness, my sometimes unruly emotions, and all the other normal challenges of life, I strive to apply everything I have recommended in this book to you. I have become convinced that there is no other way but God's way, and I want it. But I have my "moments" and yes, even my "days" when I don't completely live all I believe and preach. To put it plainly, I sin. I think the wrong way. I do the wrong thing. When this happens, I have two natural reactions—both of which I see in the lives of others as well.

Given my personality and temperament, which is sometimes described as the "accused" personality, my most common reaction is to feel like a wretch who doesn't belong in any role of influence or leadership or even in the kingdom of God for that matter. In such a state, I am vulnerable to hearing these attacks of the evil one:

> *Just give up. You'll never succeed.*
> *Quit living in a dream world. You're a born loser!*
> *Look at how hard you tried. Don't you see you will never get it right?*
> *Quit trying to be spiritual. You'll never be anything but a hypocrite.*

Paul talks about godly sorrow being a good thing that produces good fruit, but listening to such accusations doesn't bring godly sorrow. A *sorry state of sorrow* is produced—worldly not godly—and nothing good will come of wallowing in it. At such times, we are focused entirely on ourselves and not at all on the grace of God.

But there is another reaction I can and do have to my sin which is to rationalize it and make a defense for it. Like many others I have known, I am good at listing all the reasons why my situation is a very difficult one and why my actions should be excused. While I don't seem to have the basic "excused" personality, I can still make those excuses. Even though I more naturally fall into worldly sorrow and self-pity, I have those times when I get my list of trials and pressures out and present them to God and others as if to say "surely you can see I am not to blame." My normal accused personality can masquerade as humility causing those who know me to be misled and allow me to get away with these excuses. Others may be fooled, but God is not, and I will not find victory until I agree with his assessment of my situation.

My message here is simple: *If we are to be long-term overcomers, we must face and deal with our sin in a godly way.* Neither worldly sorrow nor a self-righteous defense fits that bill. What is needed is (1) a wholehearted acceptance of our responsibility for sin and (2) an equally wholehearted acceptance of God's grace and forgiveness.

Suppose you are facing a challenge—an illness, an "impossible" schedule, a character issue—and you set out to overcome with the help of God. You have some victorious days; good things happen and others are encouraged by your life. But then the heat is turned up, the temptations get stronger, and your will seems to weaken. You sin. You do the wrong thing. Maybe you lash out at someone. Maybe you indulge yourself. Maybe you just turn faithless. But there is a way out and a way up. It could look something like this:

> *Accused:* "Yes, I have taken a wrong turn. Yes, I have developed the wrong attitudes and done the wrong thing. In plain language, I have sinned again. I hear loud voices telling me to quit trying, telling me I will never succeed, telling me it's a losing battle. Emotionally I am down. My energy is sapped. I'm not sure

I can try again. I feel like a wretch. I want to give up.

But wait . . . Christ died for people like me, and his blood doesn't just cleanse us once—it cleanses again and again. By his grace, I was making progress, and by his grace, I can be forgiven and make progress again.

Father, a dozen times I may fail. A hundred times I may fall. A thousand times I may mess up, but I thank you that every time I can be forgiven and stay on that the road toward progress. Thank you for your amazing grace."

Or if your tendency is to deny your sin and defend yourself, the solution might look like this:

Excused: "I know my responses weren't very good. I know I could have done a lot better. I know what happened here is a setback in my effort to overcome. The truth is I'm not sure anyone should expect me to overcome. The pressure is just too much and, besides, I don't think anyone else really understands how tough it is to be in a situation like this. The people who are trying to help me have it so much easier than I do.

But wait. . . the Bible does say that what I did here was sin, and I really shouldn't try to get around that. I was changing and growing, but defending myself now won't help me to continue. My emotions are clamoring for me to justify my actions, but the Word of God tells me to confess my sin and somewhere I heard that means to own it—to say 'it is mine.' Any sin not properly named and owned represents a great threat to my efforts.

God, help me to call my sin by its right name, to confess it and own it and then accept your forgiveness so I can get moving again toward a victory."

Whoever you are, I know you will continue to face difficult challenges, and even with your most determined efforts to be an overcomer, you will sin. In every situation there are always two things to overcome: (1) the challenge itself and (2) our sinful reactions to the challenge. As you commit yourself to deal with the first, you will inevitably run into problems with the second. You need to know yourself well and see which of the two wrong options you are tempted to take. You absolutely need honest friends in your life who will tell you the truth, and you better do what it takes to find them.

In Revelation 12 there is a passage written in a very different age from ours, under very different circumstances, but with surprising relevance to our efforts to face sin and then move on. Pay particular attention to words that are emphasized.

Then I heard a loud voice in heaven say:
  "Now have come the salvation and the power
    and the kingdom of our God,
  and the authority of his Christ.

For *the accuser of our brothers,*
  who accuses them before our God day
    and night, has been hurled down.

> *They overcame him by the blood of the Lamb*
> *and by the word of their testimony;*
> they did not love their lives so much
> as to shrink from death
> (Revelation 12:10-11, emphasis added).

The evil one will try to use our sin in some way. He may try driving us into discouragement, as apparently is the intent here, or he may try to turn us into prideful defenders of our sin. In either case the solution is to overcome him *by the blood of the Lamb.* Our mind change may look something like this:

> "Yes, you are right. I did sin. But I'm in Christ Jesus and I'm committed to the way of the cross. I will confess my sin, repent of it and put my faith in his finished work on the cross and step out again."

Or

> "No, Satan, you are wrong. I do need to own up to my sin. There is *no* defense for sin, but there is forgiveness in Christ when I come clean about it."

No wonder Paul says Christ has set us free from the law of sin and death. Apart from Christ, there is a law—a spiritual principle: *Sin kills.* And it can kill our efforts to overcome. But through the blood of the Lamb, we can overcome sin again and again.

Envision your effort to overcome as a spiritual marathon. Imagine that you have made the final turn with the finish line only a few hundred meters away. Imagine yourself striding smoothly toward it. But then, only ten meters from the line, you take your eyes off of God and you give in to selfishness or pride. You stumble and land right on your face. You have been running for months or years to get to this moment, but now you have blown it. But here is the gospel: Whether you are ten seconds or ten years from the finish line, grace is still grace, still available and the blood of Christ still cleanses. As long as you are honest, humble and repentant, you can get up, go on, and the crown of glory will be yours!

Here is the rule: Don't ever let sin cause you to quit. It can always be faced, confessed and forgiven completely.

Chapter Eleven
The Power of Weakness

This chapter is being written at the end of a tough week. Walking and standing have been more difficult. My fatigue is deeper. There are several indicators that I may be having a new advancement of my illness. I am confronted on days like these with the reality of my weakness.

Several years ago, a time like this would have left me struggling with despair, but by the grace of God that is not where I am. Yes, I am fighting to get perspective, pondering what appointments I can and cannot keep and struggling to stay focused on my mission, but I am not in despair. This in large part is due to a different and more correct way of thinking about weakness.

You are just like me—you don't like to feel weak. You like to feel strong. You like to know what to do and you like to have the power to do it. *But weakness is a fact of human life,* and you and I will never totally escape it. The wrong view of such weakness often causes us to question our ability to overcome. For many of us, overcoming will not happen without a dramatic mind change about the whole subject of weakness. There are several things we must understand:

First, realize that God is not shocked, disgusted or irritated by the fact that we are weak. If we feel weak, we may think God is very disappointed in us. This is potentially disastrous thinking because it leaves us feeling alienated from the only one who can take us in our weakness and do something powerful with us.

Scripture reveals that there *are* things that irritate and anger God—rebellion and stubbornness and disobedience, for example. But there are a number of passages that show us his attitude toward weakness is very different. Consider this statement from the writer of Hebrews:

> Therefore, since we have a great high priest who has gone through the heavens, Jesus the Son of God, let us hold firmly to the faith we profess. For we do not have a high priest who is unable to sympathize with our weaknesses, but we have one who has been tempted in every way, just as we are—yet was without sin. Let us then approach the throne of grace with confidence, so that we may receive mercy and find grace to help us in our time of need (Hebrews 4:14-16).

Jesus' attitude toward our weakness is not condemnation. It is not impatience. It is not frustration. No, he sympathizes with us—relates to us, understands us. That certainly means he doesn't give up on us or write us off because we just don't pass muster. He took on our flesh, and he remembers what it is like to be weak, to be dog tired, to be emotionally drained. Our weaknesses are not foreign to him.

In describing for us the work of the Spirit in Romans 8, Paul lets us know that our weakness is seen as the Spirit's opportunity:

> In the same way, the Spirit helps us in our weakness. We do not know what we ought to pray for, but the Spirit himself intercedes for us with groans that words cannot express. And he who searches our hearts knows the mind of the Spirit, because the Spirit intercedes for the saints in accordance with God's will (Romans 8:26-27).

What does the Spirit do to us in our weakness? Condemn us? Ridicule us? Blast us? No, he helps! Specifically here, the reference is to our weakness in knowing how to exercise the most basic of spiritual disciplines—prayer. Sometimes, we are just too weak, in whatever way, to even pray. When that happens, my natural tendency is to feel unspiritual and even unacceptable to God. But God "knows how we are formed and he remembers that we are dust" (Psalm 103:14), and his Spirit is there to offer help in those moments.

Second, we must understand that biblical people who were great for God were often people with great struggles with weakness. Let me give you a test. Think for a moment of someone you know who is "strong for God." Suppose one day you stayed at his or her home and passed by the bedroom, only to hear this plaintive prayer: "Be merciful to me, O Lord, for I am in distress; my eyes grow weak with sorrow, my soul and my body with grief. My life is consumed by anguish and my years by groaning; my strength fails because of my affliction, and my bones grow weak." Would you be tempted to reevaluate? Would you say, " I thought this person was a strong man (or woman) of faith, but I guess not"?

Perhaps you recognize the words from the prayer. They are from Psalm 31 and written by David—the man after God's own heart. He was a man who had moments when he felt great weakness, but in his weakness he exercised faith, and God worked in his life.

What does this mean? It means just because you go through times of being spiritually low, just because you feel weak and worn down, doesn't mean you aren't spiritual and faithful. It certainly doesn't mean God cannot use you—not if you go on to say the kinds of things that David did:

> But I trust in you, O Lord;
> I say, "You are my God."
> My times are in your hands;
> deliver me from my enemies
> and from those who pursue me
> (Psalm 31:14-15).

The person of faith is not a superhero who feels no weakness, but he or she is a person who refuses to give up on God even in the midst of weakness.

If David is the Old Testament writer who is most open with us about his weakness, Paul would be his counterpart in the New Testament. He seems an unlikely candidate, given his background, but the gospel had so changed his life that he was radically open about the things he felt. Writing to a church questioning his authority, he honestly admitted:

> When I came to you, brothers, I did not come with elo-
> quence or superior wisdom as I proclaimed to you the
> testimony about God. For I resolved to know nothing
> while I was with you except Jesus Christ and him cruci-
> fied. I came to you in weakness and fear, and with much
> trembling (1 Corinthians 2:1-3).

What do you think? Should a person ever be sent to a city
to plant a church when he is feeling weakness and fear *to the
point of trembling?* God must have thought it was the right
thing to do. Paul could at the same time admit that weakness
and fear were a part of his life, and still make an impact like
few others have made because in his weakness, he relied on
God and refused to let go of his faith.

He would later wrestle with some unidentified "thorn in
the flesh" and plead with God to take it away. Whatever it
was, it made him feel weak and he wanted it out of his life.
He surely reasoned that he could do so much more without
it. But God did not take it away. Instead he told the struggling apostle, "My grace is sufficient for you, for my power is
made perfect in weakness" (2 Corinthians 12:9). This dramatic encounter with God resulted in a major mind change.
Remarkably, Paul could say after all this, "I delight in weakness. . .for when I am weak, then I am strong" (12:10). Not
only did Paul learn that weakness is acceptable, but that
through faith it can become the location of God's greatest
work.

*Third, we must be convinced that even in our weakness,
we can still respond with faith.* Hebrews 4 (noted earlier)

says that Jesus understands our weakness, but it also says that even in that state, we can "hold to the faith we profess." God may permit us to be in weakness, but he will not allow us to be in such weakness that we cannot hold onto our faith. That would be putting us into a temptation beyond what we can bear, and he will not allow that.

Several years ago on a day when I was confined to bed, I came across a great little verse in the Book of Revelation. Jesus says to the church in Philadelphia, "You have little strength, yet you have kept my word and have not denied my name" (3:8). Even when we have little strength, we can still have radical faith that gets the attention of God!

Today, around the world God will do some amazing things through people who are tired, people who are sick, people who are limited in various ways. It should not happen. It does not make worldly sense. But it happens whenever someone says, "Yes, my weaknesses are there, *but* God can use me anyway."

We may not understand how God can transform the weak into the strong. We just need to change our minds and believe that he can.

Chapter Twelve
Trouble and Joy

Pain is not pleasant. Hardships are not enjoyable. When is the last time you got up on a beautiful Saturday morning with nothing on your schedule that was pressing and said to your wife, husband or another friend, "Let's go out and see if we can find some problems today"? None of us is really interested in looking for trouble. More than enough of it has its way of finding us. We seek pleasure, fun and comfort, but not trouble. But listen as Jesus teaches us a powerful lesson about life:

> In this world you will have trouble, but take heart, I have overcome the world (John 16:33).

We need to hear him and believe him. We will never be without trouble in this world. If, in this world, we keep expecting "no trouble," if we feel we have a right to have "no trouble," if we think God is unfair anytime we have trouble, then we are setting ourselves up for frustration and bitterness.

In this world we will have trouble and all that goes with it: pain, confusion, bewilderment, disappointment and stress. We will work through some trouble, emerge from it, only to find some other form of it awaiting us. Such is life, and it could all sound quite depressing, but Jesus is telling us that all this trouble does not have to drive us to despair.

"Take heart," he says. Take heart right in the middle of the trouble because he is greater than the trouble. Take heart because no matter what the trouble, he is able to deal with it. He is able to sustain us every time and enable us to move on through it. Beyond this, he is able to use us, sometimes remarkably, in the midst of the trouble. He is able to work for our good and the good of others even when there is trouble.

But is this only theory? I am writing these words on a day when physically I am quite depleted. Two physically and emotionally challenging weeks have taken their toll. A good night's sleep hasn't done much to relieve the fatigue. My legs are stubbornly refusing to work. The pain is persistent. Stacks of papers on the desk at my office (including a deadline for this book) call urgently for my attention. Other stacks of bills, business papers and ministry needs on my desk here at home are making the same appeal. (Little wonder that I've changed the words to a familiar hymn to "No Stacks in Heaven.") As I see the many needs and contemplate my own limitations, I sense a bit of the darkness we call depression trying to sneak back into my soul. Life's challenges are looking pretty big. I am feeling pretty small, and this is not fun.

But then I recall Jesus' words: "In this world, you will have trouble, but take heart, I have overcome the world." Yes, I remind myself, there is trouble. Each day has its own, but once again today, as I have on hundreds of other days, I can take heart because I am with the one who has overcome. I don't know how it will all get done, but whether it does or doesn't, I know he has written my name in heaven. I can't see how to resolve every problem and meet every need, but I do know he works for good in everything. My challenges are still real, but they look quite different when laid at the mouth of the empty tomb.

As I think about him, I am taking heart. The legs aren't any better, the pain and the fatigue are still there, but hope and courage are returning. The darkness is being pushed out and sealed off. I'm starting to look forward to what is ahead. I think that's what he had in mind when he spoke these words.

The life of an overcomer is a mixture of pain and joy, trouble and hope, trial and love. The pain, troubles and trials give us the opportunity to show the supremacy of the joy, hope and love that comes from God. Throughout John 15 and 16, as Jesus gives final words to his disciples before his death, he alternately talks of grief and joy, trouble and peace. In the life of a disciple, there will be both sides of the coin, but ultimate reality is on our side. At the final gun, when the game ends, our team will be the winner. Our captain will be the most valuable player, and we will all share together with him the fruits of victory.

Pain is not going to go away. In this world we will have it. Some of us will likely have more of it in the future than we have had in the past. But in the midst of the pain, we can change our minds. We can fix our minds on Jesus and his victory. We can lock our minds onto his presence with us. And however great the trouble or the pain, we can be filled with a joy that overcomes. We can simultaneously be in the midst of trouble and full of joy. Thanks be to God who alone can give us such a victory!

Chapter Thirteen
Love and Laughter

As I worked to finish up the second edition of this book, I asked myself if I had left out anything that had been particularly helpful to me. Of course, the answer was that there was much more that could be said about how to be an overcomer. After all, this is a pretty slim volume. However, two things came to mind very quickly, and I felt I would be remiss not to write about them, if only briefly. These two things are love and laughter.

The Liberation of Love

Whenever we are faced with a stiff challenge—a chronic illness, constant pain, a big loss, an overwhelming problem—there is an even greater temptation than normal to turn inward, to think of ourselves, to focus on our need for relief. Natural thinking says, "Look out for Number One, focus on what you want, express frustration about what you are not getting or how tough life has become."

I recently spoke with someone going through something very difficult. I asked him how he wanted to handle a certain change that challenging circumstances had dictated. "As painlessly as possible," he said. "I've been through enough." This person has lived a life of giving to others, but in that comment he revealed the weakness we all have in the face of strong natural feelings. His pain was causing him to feel a bit like a victim—a victim who had suffered enough. Like Job, he had run a good race but was becoming weary in the battle. Like Job, he may have been thinking, "This doesn't seem fair." In the days that followed, this person did not stay at this point. He read Scripture, he prayed, and he did not stop giving; but his words reminded me that the pull toward self is extremely strong.

I don't know anyone who does not face such temptations. How often I have struggled with thinking that I should not have to give or serve because of my own limitations. Some of you are reading this book because you are going through something that is as tough as anything you have ever faced. There is a powerful temptation to think primarily about yourself and to excuse yourself from your responsibility to others. But we must change our minds. We must realize that nothing helps us to overcome any more than the deliberate decision to love others and give to them whatever we have to give.

In saying this, we have come to the very heart of Christian teaching. "Deny yourself and take up your cross daily and follow me," said Jesus. Crucify, put to death, execute self-centered thinking. This was the center of his message. If you try to save your life (by focusing on yourself and waging a campaign of self-protection), you will lose it. But, Jesus went on to say that if you lose your life for my sake (that is, give up yourself for a higher mission of loving God and loving others), then you will find it. This is a spiritual truth, an unalterable, immutable spiritual law.

When I am going through something that tests my mettle and tries my soul, I certainly will have to put time and energy into resolving certain issues. But I must never let what I am facing distract me from my calling, and that is to love others—to think about them, their needs, their hurts and to ask God to use me, even if I am wounded, to build them up, to guide them, to encourage them and to help them.

Two biblical pictures jump into my mind: First, Jesus on the eve of his crucifixion, his darkest day, washing the disciples' feet. Second, Jesus on the cross, feeling the physical pain of the torture and the emotional anguish of abandonment, but telling John to take care of his mother. Jesus understood love, and he understood that we must stay committed to showing it even when powerful forces are telling us to think, "But what about *me?*"

We need to understand the liberation of love. Love—that decision to take our eyes off of ourselves and put them on others—liberates us from the ugly prison of selfishness where so many stay locked up. Whatever we are facing, we will handle it better if we take the time and effort to show love.

Yes, we may be tired. Yes, we may have pain. Yes, we may feel we deserve a break. But *the fruit of the Spirit is love.* That means we can cry out to God and receive the help of the Spirit so we can give what we can, and in giving we will receive.

The Lift of Laughter

Some years ago it never would have occurred to me to include a section on laughter in a book on overcoming. I would have viewed overcoming as far too serious a matter. I was a serious person, and dealing with difficult issues is serious business. But the more I have lived and the more I have learned, the more I see laughter as one of the gifts that God has given to help us win victories.

Sure, some people need to be more serious. They take everything lightly. They joke their way through life and use laughter as a way to avoid really resolving painful issues that need to be worked through more thoughtfully and soberly. There is a time to turn our laughter into mourning (James 4:9). There is a time to stop laughing, to be convicted, to mourn over sin and to make serious commitments to live differently. But there are other people more like I was who don't understand that laughter can be used to lighten the load, give a needed respite from heavy life-matters or even give some needed perspective.

Lorretta LaRoche is a humorist here in the Boston area. The message of her popular video, *The Joy of Stress*, is that we will all do a lot better with life if we learn to laugh. She talks humorously about how many people tend to "catastrophize" and "awfulize" about their circumstances. Her imitations of people who do this help us all to laugh at ourselves. But she has a point. Many of us are "catastrophizers" and "awfulizers." Instead of painting a gloomy picture, we need to learn to laugh.

My friend Bill Sullivan, who also has MS, has worked effectively for years with physically challenged Christians. I have often said that part of his effectiveness comes from his great sense of humor. I once told him he was my favorite sit-down comic. His ability to laugh about his illness, loss of coordination, memory lapses and the like not only helps him but helps others get perspective on their challenges.

But overall, wouldn't you say that the Bible is a serious book? One of my daughters recently gave me a Dilbert book for Christmas. I laughed out loud through half a plane ride as I read the conversations between this nerdy fellow and his little friend—Dogbert. But the Bible is a very different book. You don't see many people laughing as they read the Bible. Yet, Scripture says some significant things that let us know that laughter and humor must not be overlooked as a part of a balanced life.

After laughing originally from disbelief, Sarah, the wife of Abraham, eventually came to laugh in a most positive way about her young son born in her old age. "Sarah said, 'God has brought me laughter, and everyone who hears about this will laugh with me'" (Genesis 21:6). Instead of "catastrophizing" about the trials of advanced-age motherhood, she learned to laugh. She didn't burden her friends with her situation. She brought some laughter into their lives.

For many of us this kind of response requires a major mind change. We tend to "awfulize" and see the heaviness of burdens and the impossibility of problems. We find little humor in our trials. The Scriptures do say that "there is a time to laugh" (Ecclesiastes 3:4), but some of us think that time could only be when everything is going great. Since that doesn't happen very often, the times we laugh are few and far between.

We do need to change our minds. We need to be reminded that no matter what happens, God is still working for good in the lives of those who love him. We need to understand that laughing in our trials is a way of showing faith that a good outcome awaits us. If the reunion of the Jews in Jerusalem after a difficult exile caused them to have "mouths filled with laughter" (Psalm 126:2), what should we expect will be true of our reunion in heaven? And if we are very shortly going to be laughing through eternity, why not start now?

"All the days of the oppressed are wretched," reads Proverbs 15:15, "but the cheerful heart has a continual feast." My understanding of this is that every day is pretty miserable for the person who views life as burdensome and oppressive, but even the toughest days are happy for the person with a cheerful heart. Two people going through the very same thing can view the experience in very different ways, but how they view it makes all the difference. One will be beaten down; the other will overcome.

"A cheerful heart is good medicine," reads Proverbs 17:22, "but a crushed spirit dries up the bones." *Reader's Digest* has carried a monthly feature for years titled "Laughter: The Best Medicine." As one who deals with a chronic illness, I have learned how true this is. To laugh in general is healthy. To laugh even at some of the things we must "endure," helps lighten the load. (It sure beats "awfulizing"!) To laugh in anticipation of an ultimate victory is probably the best medicine of all.

There is a way in which love and laughter belong together. One of the most encouraging things you do for other people is to bring some cheer into their lives. If you do this *as they see you facing a trial*, you will not only make them laugh, you will inspire them! You will overcome, and you will help them to do the same.

Chapter Fourteen
The Rest of This Book

Much of what comes in the next section was actually written first and has had a powerful impact on me. These thoughts were written down in the midst of my own struggle to overcome. I would describe myself as a person who naturally thinks negatively. I am one of those people who looks at the glass that is half-full and sees it as half-empty. In my purely natural state, negative thoughts steadily trickle into my mind when I'm at my best and cascade like a waterfall when I'm at my worst. Take that natural man and combine him with a frustrating, unpredictable, debilitating illness like MS, and you can guess what you would get. But thank God the man who got MS also had a Bible, and as he used that Bible he found (and is still finding) keys to overcoming.

Knowing God has not stopped negative or unspiritual thoughts from appearing on the screen of my mind, but knowing God has given me some very important say about whether they stay there or whether something else replaces them. What you will find in the rest of this book is the right kind of thoughts I wrote down to replace the wrong ones. These are the thoughts I go back to again and again, and it is on these thoughts that I seek to lock my focus.

In some cases, I have focused on these truths so much that I feel they have finally become part of me. But I think I know better than to be prideful about that. A new and harder hit from life may very well have me reaching again to grasp what I thought I already had. In other cases, I'm still working to get these truths deep in my heart. But in all cases, I find I am worlds better off meditating on these thoughts than on the negative ones that so naturally come my way. After writing many of these down and using them over a period of months, one day I wrote at the end of them, "Thank God for these thoughts." I knew they had made a powerful difference in my life. I knew God had used them to help me keep giving and serving and believing. I knew that, for me, they were gifts from God to meet various needs in my life. And so I share them with you, with a prayer that they will help you, too, to be an overcomer.

How to Use These Thoughts

1. As you read these thoughts, keep in mind that most were written in response to some negative thought I had and was tempted to cultivate. I have not written those negative thoughts out because (1) I didn't write them down at the time and cannot remember them all and (2) you will be most impacted if you think of what thoughts in your life most need to be replaced.

2. I would encourage you to make this something of a workbook. You may eventually find that your personal notes will come to mean even more to you than the thoughts I have written.

3. If you don't seem to relate to one of the thoughts,

move on to another. The one you skipped may mean more another day.

4. I would strongly advise you *not* to skim through these but instead to exercise discipline the first time through and focus on one each day. I came to them one at a time and found the most force came from meditating on them carefully one at a time. In going back to them, I often pick two or three that seem most appropriate for what I am facing.

5. Do look up the scriptures on each page. Seeing the biblical authority for such thoughts can only strengthen your faith in their validity and power. "The word of God is living and active."

6. Warning: Never think that the short thoughts found here can replace serious in-depth Bible study. These thoughts should not be seen as easy-to-swallow pills that do away with the need for spiritual meals. You will become an overcomer as you wrestle with circumstances and with the Scriptures and emerge with God's truth that speaks powerfully to your situation. Let these thoughts just be examples of how to do that.

7. Understand that the decision to put these in print did not come because of any feeling that they are complete. Even as this book goes to press, I will be adding to my list. My hope is that this book will encourage you to develop your personal list of thoughts you most need. A few pages have been left at the end for you to get started.

8. Finally, understand that the promises included in these thoughts are *the privileges of those in the kingdom of God.*

Not just anyone, for example, can be sure that God is at work for good in all things in his life. The Bible says that promise is *only* for those who love God and are called according to his purpose (Romans 8:28). These assurances can only be claimed by those who have died with Christ to an old life and are continuing in their faith (Romans 6:1-4; Colossians 1:22-23). If that is your situation, rejoice and read on! If it is not, seek, and you, too, can find.

> "To him who overcomes, I will give the right to sit with me on my throne, just as I overcame and sat down with my Father on his throne" (Revelation 3:21).

POWER THOUGHTS

1

*I*n every situation
there is a right and spiritual
way to think.

It may take me some time to find it.
It may take some discipline to embrace it.
But it is always there, and it is always best.
It is always the key
to overcoming any challenge.

PHILIPPIANS 1:27
EPHESIANS 5:10
1 THESSALONIANS 5:16-18

2

God is in control.

Today. . .tomorrow. . .forever.
God is God.
Nothing is outside his sovereignty.
He cannot lose control.
He is never surprised or unprepared.
God never asks,
"What are we going to do now?"

PSALM 2:2-6
PSALM 90:2
ISAIAH 50:7

3

*G*od will provide.

No matter what the need.
He cares.
He allows us to have needs.
He sees our needs.
He meets them all.

ISAIAH 58:11
MATTHEW 6:28-34
PHILIPPIANS 4:19

4

*A*ccept whatever comes…with faith.

Disappointment? Faith.
Unfairness? Faith.
Fear? Faith.
Temptation? Faith.
Opportunity? Faith.
Victory? Faith.

GALATIANS 5:6
HEBREWS 11:8, 11, 13
1 JOHN 5:4

5

*W*astes:
regret, wishing, worry.

Be smart. Don't use time for any of these.
No regret—accept forgiveness.
No wishing—bloom where you are planted.
No worry—trust God who is not perplexed at all.

MATTHEW 6:27

6

*H*elps:
faith, thanksgiving,
determination.

Faith inspires you.
Thanksgiving gives you perspective.
Determination keeps you moving.

2 THESSALONIANS 1:11
PHILIPPIANS 4:6
LUKE 9:51

7

*P*ray: "Father, not my will but yours be done."

Nothing is more right to do than this.
Nothing is so purifying and so liberating.
Nothing is so like Christ.

MATTHEW 26:36-44

8

There is much more
to life than your problem.

It may be loud.
It may shout for attention.
It may seem unbearable.
But God is greater.

2 CORINTHIANS 4:16-18
ROMANS 8:18
PHILIPPIANS 2:4

9

*B*e thankful. Laugh. Sing. Trust God.

Apply this today.
Apply it every day.
Yes, even with what is happening today.
Don't let any new development stop you.

1 THESSALONIANS 5:16-18
PROVERBS 31:25
PSALM 147:7
JOHN 14:1

10

*J*oy, not suffering, will be eternal.

Pain is bearable when it leads to something.
We are on our way to everlasting joy.
"The toils of the road will seem nothing
when we get to the end of the way."

ISAIAH 51:11
ISAIAH 61:7
ROMANS 8:18-21

11

"God is with you, mighty warrior."

Who, me? Yes, you!
But I am the weakest of the weak.
So what?
God loves to be with the weak.
Remember Gideon.

JUDGES 6

12

Humility is the most powerful force in the world.

God loves it.
God honors it.
God blesses it.
With it, you cannot lose.
You can have it in all circumstances.

LUKE 14:11
JAMES 3:13-18
JAMES 4:6
1 PETER 5:5

13

Relax.
Your God reigns.

PSALM 47:8
PSALM 93:1
ISAIAH 52:7

14

*S*piritual truth is greater than physical circumstances.

The physical is temporary; the spiritual is eternal.
More obvious does not mean more real.
The eternal is superior to the temporary.

ROMANS 8:17
2 CORINTHIANS 4:16-18
HEBREWS 10:32-34

15

In all things God works for your good.

No exceptions and no lapses.
Even in what happened yesterday.
Even in something that caused great pain.
Even in something that dashed your hopes.
All things means *all* things.

ISAIAH 49:15-16
JEREMIAH 29:11
ROMANS 8:28

16

*I*n Christ you are: Gifted. Forgiven. Assigned. Valuable. Secure.

You may hear other "tapes."
But this is the truth.
It is true after a bad day as much as
after a good day.

EPHESIANS 4:7-8
ROMANS 8:1
1 CORINTHIANS 7:17
LUKE 12:24
JOHN 10:28

17

*N*ever
lose your dream.

If one gets taken away,
seek another one.
God is not through with you.
He still has plans.
When he closes one door,
he opens another.

ACTS 16:6-10

18

No complaining!

None!
Not about anyone.
Not about anything.
Address problems and find solutions,
but don't complain.

PHILIPPIANS 2:14
PHILIPPIANS 4:8-9
1 PETER 4:9

19

*B*e "unreasonably,"
"illogically" joyful because
*your name is written
in heaven.*

It seems you have more to do than
you can get done...but
your name is written in heaven.
Your prayers didn't get answered the
way you thought they would...but
your name is written in heaven.
You are having "one of those days"...but
your name is written in heaven.
You didn't do everything right...but
your name is written in heaven."

LUKE 10:18-20

20

$\mathcal{D}$ecide to
enjoy the challenge.

If it is going to be there,
you might as well enjoy it.
God is allowing it for some good purpose.
Like Jacob, don't let go of it
until it blesses you.

GENESIS 32:22-28
JAMES 1:2-4

21

$\mathcal{C}$hoose your mood.

If the one you have right now is not right,
you can exchange it.
Don't allow the "wrong side of the
bed" to control your life.

DEUTERONOMY 30:19-20
JOSHUA 24:15
PSALM 119:30

22

*E*very frustration is an opportunity for faith.

Don't whine. Don't explode.
Pray. Look for God.
Be assured that he is near
and ready to work.

ACTS 16:6-10
PHILIPPIANS 4:4-7

*M*orning breath of the soul? Rinse it!

Waking up with the blahs?
Feeling unmotivated, uninspired,
discouraged, depressed?
Dreading some things you have to do?
Take prayer and the Word and deal with it!
Say "This is not of God;
I won't stand for it."

PSALM 5:3
PSALM 42:5
HEBREWS 12:1-2

24

*H*e arose!

That changes everything!
How different does
your problem look when placed
at the mouth of the
empty tomb?

ROMANS 8:11
1 CORINTHIANS 15:12-20
1 PETER 3:21-22

25

*D*on't resent the
spiritual battle.

Be thankful you
have the weapons to fight it.
Be glad you are
on the winning side.

2 CORINTHIANS 10:3-5
EPHESIANS 6:10-18
REVELATION 22:1-5

*M*ake someone feel loved *today*.

Get out of yourself.
Put your problems in perspective by
meeting another's need.
Power comes when you give.

1 CORINTHIANS 13
PHILIPPIANS 2:3-4
1 JOHN 3:16-20

27

*M*ake a list of 100 things for which you are thankful.

"Count your many blessings; name them one by one."
You may be surprised how many you have been overlooking.

PSALM 100:4
COLOSSIANS 2:6-7
HEBREWS 12:28-29

28

Know what most threatens your dedication to Christ...then nail it!

Identify it. Confess it.
Ask others to pray about it.
Whatever you do,
overcome it.

MATTHEW 5:29
1 TIMOTHY 5:11
HEBREWS 12:1-2

God has not given you too much.

If you must face something,
you can face it.
If you must change something,
you can change it.
If you must overcome something,
you can overcome it.

"When something must be done, there is no use
talking about whether or not it can be done."
(C.S. Lewis)

1 CORINTHIANS 10:13

Give thanks to the God
"who daily bears our
burdens."

Whatever yours is today,
he can carry it.
For him, it is just
"another day at the office."

PSALM 68:19

*T*here is no condemnation for you who are in Christ Jesus.

Are you perfect? No.
Are you in Christ? Yes.
Is he your Lord? Yes.
Are you totally forgiven?
Absolutely.

ROMANS 8:1

32

*N*othing on earth
(or in the heavens)
can separate you from the
love of Christ.

Not pain. Not loss.
Not grief. Not abuse. Not rejection.
Not disappointment. Not failure.
Nothing.

ROMANS 8:35-39

*B*loom where you are planted.

"We are not here to wish to be somewhere or something we are not, but to do the thing that pleases him, exactly where we are and as we are."
(Amy Carmichael)

1 CORINTHIANS 7:23-24

34

*Y*ou are shielded by
God's power.

Anything that hits you,
you can handle with God's power.
Anything too much for you,
God keeps out.

1 PETER 1:3-9

35

*T*rouble is often the ground where God cultivates some of his best crops.

No trouble is bigger than God.
No trouble is stronger than God.
No trouble overwhelms God.

GENESIS 50:20
GALATIANS 4:13
PHILIPPIANS 1:12-14

36

*F*ind out what pleases
the Lord.

Seek it.
Desire it.
What pleases him
will be best for you.

EPHESIANS 5:10

37

*P*ray: "God, do
something powerful in spite
of my weakness."

Such a prayer shows humility,
demonstrates faith and honors God.
He will be delighted to bless it.

2 CORINTHIANS 12:9

38

When you suffer, never ask:
"Why me?" Instead ask:
"How can I show faith, hope and
love in this situation?"

There will always be a good answer.
Righteousness in the midst of suffering
shines all the more brightly.

ACTS 6:11-15
ACTS 7:54-60

39

When you sin, confess. Don't defend.

Failure won't stop you,
if you keeping walking in the light.
Transgression won't ruin you,
if you stay open...with God and
with others.

1 JOHN 1:8-10
JAMES 5:16

40

Forgive as God has forgiven you.

Forgive quickly.
Forgive completely.
Realize nothing will hurt you
like not forgiving others.

MATTHEW 6:14-15
EPHESIANS 4:31-32

41

Enlarge your view of God.

If he doesn't look big enough to
overcome your problem,
you don't see him clearly.

2 KINGS 6:15-17
ISAIAH 40:10-15
ISAIAH 40:18-26

42

*W*hoever gives up on God always gives up too soon.

He doesn't wear your watch.
He doesn't use your datebook.
He doesn't always follow your script.
But he always comes through.

2 CORINTHIANS 1:18-20

43

$\mathcal{D}$on't ever lose your
sense of humor.

"A cheerful heart is
good medicine, but a crushed spirit
dries up the bones."

PROVERBS 17:22
ECCLESIASTES 3:4

44

*I*t is God's will for
you to totally trust him and
to be completely at peace in
every situation.

You will have to *learn* this.
It took Paul some time to learn this
(compare 2 Corinthians 1 with Philippians 4).
It will take you time to learn it.
Just decide that you will learn it.

PHILIPPIANS 4:4-7, 12-13

45

*W*ith God, there is
no straw that breaks the
camel's back.

You may think, "I can't take one more thing."
But with God you always can.
You can take whatever he allows life to bring.
He will always be enough.

PSALM 34:17-19
1 PETER 5:10-11

46

*J*ust live the next thirty minutes by faith.

This one you need for the really tough days.
This one is for the days when life
seems most impossible.
Thirty minutes of all-out faith can
change your mind about a whole day.

ROMANS 4:18-21

47

You ou may be challenged *and* weak, but you can still have radical faith.

Never think radical faith is only for the strong.
Faith is most radical when it seems most unlikely.

MATTHEW 9:20-22
MARK 7:24-30
REVELATION 3:8

48

Celebrate every victory.

Small victories? Celebrate!
Big victories? Celebrate!
Celebrating is God's plan
and a way of building for more victories.
Plan a victory today and then celebrate it.

2 CHRONICLES 30

49

*G*od always gives the next
grace for the next step.

It may look bigger than any you
have taken before. But if he calls you to take it,
his grace will be sufficient.
The challenges that are coming up
may be greater than any you have faced,
but God will always be enough

EXODUS 14:21-22
JUDGES 6:14
2 CORINTHIANS 1:10
PHILIPPIANS 4:13

50

*N*ever quit!

You may feel like quitting.
You may think there is no other option.
But there always is.
Decide now, and again and again,
that you will never quit.

1 CORINTHIANS 15:58
GALATIANS 6:9
2 CORINTHIANS 4:1,16

OTHER BOOKS FROM
DISCIPLESHIP PUBLICATIONS INTERNATIONAL

THE DAILY POWER SERIES
Series Editors: Thomas and Sheila Jones

Thirty Days at the Foot of the Cross
A study of the central issue of Christianity

First...the Kingdom
A study of the Sermon on the Mount

The Mission
The inspiring task of the church in every generation

Teach Us to Pray
A study of the most vital of all spiritual disciplines

To Live Is Christ
An interactive study of the Letter to the Philippians

Glory in the Church
God's plan to shine through his church

The Heart of a Champion
Spiritual inspiration from Olympic athletes

Jesus with the People
Encountering the heart and character of Jesus

PRACTICAL EXPOSITION SERIES

Life to the Full
A study of the writings of James, Peter, John and Jude
by Douglas Jacoby

Mine Eyes Have Seen the Glory
The victory of the Lamb in the Book of Revelation
by Gordon Ferguson

Power in Weakness
Second Corinthians and the Ministry of Paul
by Marty Wooten

The God Who Dared
Genesis: From Creation to Babel
by Douglas Jacoby

The Call of the Wise
An Introduction and Topical Index to the Book of Proverbs
by G. Steve Kinnard

ADDITIONAL BOOKS

The Victory of Surrender
An in-depth study of a powerful biblical concept
(workbook and tapes also available)
by Gordon Ferguson

True and Reasonable
Evidences for God in a skeptical world
by Douglas Jacoby

Friends and Lovers
by Sam and Geri Laing

Friends and Lovers Study Guide
by Mitch and Jan Mitchell

Raising Awesome Kids in Troubled Times
by Sam and Geri Laing

Let It Shine: A Devotional Book for Teens
edited by Thomas and Sheila Jones

ESPECIALLY FOR WOMEN

She Shall Be Called Woman
Volume I: Old Testament Women
Volume II: New Testament Women
edited by Sheila Jones and Linda Brumley

The Fine Art of Hospitality
edited by Sheila Jones
The Fine Art of Hospitality Handbook
edited by Sheila Jones and Betty Dyson
(two-volume set)

Our Beginning: Genesis Through the Eyes of a Woman
by Kay Summers McKean

For information about ordering these and many other resources
from DPI, call 1-888-DPI-BOOK or from outside the
U.S. 617-938-7396.

World Wide Web
http://www.dpibooks.com